POSITIVE SCHOOL CULTURE & EFFECTIVE LEADERSHIP

WORKING TOGETHER FOR GREAT RESULTS

DR MICHAEL STEWART

Published in 2025 by Amba Press, Melbourne, Australia
www.ambapress.com.au

© 2025 Michael Stewart

All rights reserved. No part of this book may be reproduced or transmitted in any form or by any means, electronic or mechanical, including photocopying, recording or by any information storage and retrieval system, without prior permission in writing from the publisher.

Previously published in 2017 by Hawker Brownlow Education.

This edition replaces all previous editions.

ISBN: 9781923215627 (pbk)
ISBN: 9781923215634 (ebk)

A catalogue record for this book is available from the National Library of Australia.

PRAISE FOR POSITIVE SCHOOL CULTURE & EFFECTIVE LEADERSHIP: WORKING TOGETHER FOR GREAT RESULTS

I congratulate Michael on his extensive and timely research into the connections between developing a positive school culture and effective leadership.

That such a coupling leads to great results is something educators have always understood intrinsically. Michael's research vivifies that belief with data that draws on the research of many in the educational field.

He addresses the increasing demands on principals' time and expertise to be many things in a school community without losing sight that the principal's role as a leader of learning must be paramount.

In this easily accessible, very readable book he provides the practical know-how to turn the book's title into a reality. Great work Michael.

Pam Betts
Executive Director Catholic Education
Archdiocese of Brisbane

Michael walks the talk when it comes to building a great school culture! His insights into this vital aspect of school leadership make great reading!

Steve Francis
Leading educator and leadership expert

As both a former colleague, and a fellow school principal, I commend Michael for the insightful and important body of work he has produced in this book.

Quality leadership and, more particularly, quality school leadership, is absolutely essential if young Australians everywhere are to reach their full potential in our schools. In drawing out the critical relationship between the principal's leadership and the nurturing of a positive school culture, Michael gets to the heart of what matters most in the disbursement of one's time and energy as a leader.

In a comprehensive manner, the work details the key behaviours of an effective school leader and, so often, this will involve forming and sustaining strong relationships to empower everyone in the school community.

In what must surely be one of the most rewarding vocations in life, this book will be wonderfully encouraging to school leaders and, importantly, those aspiring to leadership roles in our schools.

Yours in leadership,

Dr Alan Campbell
Headmaster
Anglican Church Grammar School (Churchie)

Positive School Culture and Effective Leadership

Congratulations Dr Michael Stewart on an extensive exploration of school culture, its undeniable link to school performance and the work of a school principal. This book provides so many insightful suggestions and questions for school leaders to reflect about the development of a positive school culture. I particularly like the reflective questions and decisive actions section at the end of each chapter. The generation of a positive school culture instrument provides a pragmatic tool to further assist school principals in their complex roles.

Dr Stewart has artfully grounded and linked these in an extensive examination of relevant theory supported by the 'voice' of the practitioner.

Dr Stephen Brown
Director of The Brown Collective

It is very pleasing to acknowledge the valuable contribution Michael has made to educational leadership through the writing of this book. Based on his current educational research and the practical application of his work within his own school community, Michael has captured some of the essential components to enhancing student learning within any school environment.

Among an ever-increasingly complex educational environment, Michael's practical advice for principals, and members of leadership teams, will be welcomed and greatly valued. With every positive culture, there needs to also be assurance that student learning is the core business of school communities. Michael has achieved this balance and his book is testimony to this important connection.

I congratulate Michael on this publication and know that it will serve as a valuable resource for many current and future leaders in our schools.

Leesa Jeffcoat AM | Director
Catholic Education – Diocese of Rockhampton

In this practical and engaging text, Michael Stewart reminds school leaders of the powerful role they play in creating the positive school culture necessary for school improvement and student success. School leaders have complex roles as relationship builders, visionaries, change agents and instructional leaders. Michael provides research-informed insights and hands-on strategies for navigating these multi-layered responsibilities while never losing sight of the importance of building a positive, engaged and welcoming school community with people and learning at its heart.

Joel Buchholz
Principal
Pimlico State High School

Foreword

There is a growing body of research concerning the important role of the school principal in cultivating a positive school culture. School culture influences all happenings in a school and therefore impacts on a school community and on an individual's behaviour, expectations and interactions with others. It follows that cultivating and sustaining a positive school culture should be one of the highest priorities for all school principals. To improve schools and student learning, you must first focus on the culture of the school.

This book explores the journey of a school principal in creating a positive school culture and presents research findings from a case study that explored the cultivation of a positive school culture from the viewpoint of the principal and the various stakeholders within the school. The results from this research indicate that the principal plays a pivotal and crucial role in the cultivation of a positive school culture. However, the results also demonstrated that the principal cannot do this alone, as many other members of the school community contribute to a school's culture. The principal's success in cultivating a school culture was found to depend upon his ability to unite the school community to work together to achieve the school's goals and vision. Results from the research indicated that the principal needed to use a range of strategies to cultivate and maintain a positive school culture.

> *Principals are indispensable. They are like a painter in that they colour the whole system by their actions and words and where they put their emphases and energy. They are a vital aspect. They might not be terribly conspicuous in regard to activity but behind the scenes, their input and how they drive things has a significant influence on what happens. (Principal)*

Acknowledgements

My aim for this book is to assist schools in creating positive school cultures. I hope the following pages will provide some assistance for people who wish to make a difference in their own workplace.

I would like to thank my Principal Supervisor, Professor John Dekkers. His personal commitment and honest critiques gave me the guidance to complete my research. I wish to acknowledge Associate Supervisor, Professor Bruce Knight, who believed in me from the start and provided guidance and support during my journey. I was very fortunate to have had both supervisors and will always be grateful for their support, wisdom and assistance during this dissertation process.

I express my gratitude to the principal of the school that was surveyed in this dissertation, Jim Ford, who showed much interest and support. Allowing me to research his school's community and his role in cultivating a positive culture was a very generous gesture. His positive leadership and unfailing commitment to the children in his care is an example for all school leaders. I extend my appreciation to the participants who agreed to be interviewed and completed surveys at the school at which this research was conducted. Their opinions about the topic have provided the rich data which contribute to my research. I would like to thank my colleagues. Many of the ideas that I learnt from the research I applied to my own workplace. Thank you for your words of encouragement. I also acknowledge and thank the Director of Catholic Education, Leesa Jeffcoat, for allowing me to conduct this research at one of the Catholic schools in the Diocese of Rockhampton.

I would like to acknowledge my parents, John and Pauline, who gave me the encouragement and belief to follow my dreams. To my brothers, John, Mark, Tony and Paul; brother-in-law Keith; sisters-in-law Kate, Jenny, Gai and Michelle for their words of support.

Finally, I must thank my beautiful wife Denise, for her unquestionable love, faith, patience and support that has enabled me to complete this work. She has provided the strength and belief I have needed. I would also thank my children, Matty, Tashy and Simon, for their patience and understanding. They will be almost as delighted as I am that my research has finally ended. May they apply the virtue of persistence to their own learning journey and continue to make a positive difference to all that they meet. Thank you to all.

Chapter Outlines

Chapter 1: Introduction and the Research Context

This initial chapter introduces the research topic and provides the rationale for undertaking the research. The research aims, objectives and the research questions are presented. This chapter establishes the research context and considers some of the major challenges facing education in Queensland. The school's history, characteristics and the principal's role are considered.

Chapter 2: Literature Review

This chapter presents a review of the literature that informs the research. The review covers and defines what culture is; describes the principal's role in cultivating a positive school culture and identifies some of the strategies a school principal may use to cultivate a positive school culture.

Chapter 3: Discussion of Results

This chapter provides a discussion of the results.

Chapter 4: Conclusions and Recommendations

This chapter provides conclusions from the research and considers recommendations for the school principal in cultivating a positive school culture.

Chapter 5: Positive Culture Improvement Tool

This chapter will present the Positive Culture Improvement Tool. This tool provides the many different strategies that the school community recommended would assist in the cultivation of a positive school culture to enhance school performance. The Positive Culture Improvement Tool can assist school communities to examine their own culture as the strategies presented can be used as indicators of a positive culture.

Effective leaders are reflective thinkers and take the time to reflect about how their actions and words impact on those people they lead. You will be asked questions and consider actions in relation to what you have just read.

Contents

Chapter 1 Introduction and Research Context 1
1.1 Introduction 1
1.2 Background 2
1.3 Purpose of the Book 4
1.4 Research Aims 5
1.5 The Research Site and Context 5
1.6 Education Issues and Challenges for School Principals 9
1.7 Leadership framework 12
1.8 Summary 15

Chapter 2 Review of Literature When Exploring School Culture 17
2.1 Defining School Culture 17
2.2 Benefits of Cultivating a Positive Culture Within a School Setting 22
2.3 The Principal's Role and Practices in Cultivating a Positive School Culture ... 28
2.4 Strategies a Principal may use to Promote a Positive School Culture ... 35
2.5 Summary and Conclusion 41

Chapter 3 Discussion of Results 43
3.1 Introduction 43
3.2 What Aspects of a School and School Community Contributes to a Positive School Culture? 44
3.3 Discussion of Research Question 2 54
3.4 Discussion of Research Question 3 59
3.5 Discussion of Research Question 4 64
3.6 Discussion of Research Question 5 71
3.7 Discussion of Research Question 6 78

Chapter 4 Conclusions and Recommendations 85
4.1 Introduction 85
4.2 Conclusions 85
4.3 The Key Behaviours of the Principal that Assist with the Cultivation of a Positive School Culture. 86
4.4 The Key Actions Suggested by the School Community that Can Assist with the Cultivation of a Positive School Culture 90
4.5 Recommendations for the Cultivation and Maintenance of a Positive School Culture 93
4.6 Concluding Remarks 98

Chapter 5 The Positive School Culture Improvement Tool 99
5.1 Introduction 99
5.2 Summary 111

Appendices 113
About the Author 125
References 127

Chapter 1
Introduction and Research Context

1.1 Introduction

I took a deep breath as I put down the phone. I had just accepted a principal appointment knowing that the school I was to lead had several significant challenges. For instance, the school's enrolment had dropped by 30% in four years, and there were significant behaviour challenges from the students. There was talk in the community that the school was going to be closed. As the third principal at the school in two years, my first challenge was to somehow stop the number of families leaving. My goal was to increase enrolments by being the top-performing school in the region. Therefore, I wanted to know what the specific strategies a principal could use to improve performance were.

In this respect, Deal and Peterson (2002) believe that a key factor for a school's success in promoting staff and student learning is for the principal to understand and shape the culture. They stress that a positive school culture assists in successful teaching and student learning. In order to change the school culture effectively, the principal must have a good understanding of the culture within their school (Fullan, 2009). To improve the performance of the school I needed to understand the leadership behaviours that promote a positive school culture.

I started to examine the literature about schools that had positive cultures and were achieving great results. The literature suggested that schools with positive cultures have the following attributes:
- strong community support (Engels, Horton, Devos, Bouckenooghe & Aelterman, 2008);
- promoting a positive school culture was a priority (Habeggar, 2008);
- collegiality among staff (Marzano, Waters & McNulty, 2005; Fullan, 2010);
- a rich sense of history and purpose (Deal & Peterson, 1999);
- a shared vision and strong moral purpose (O'Mahony et. al., 2006; Fullan, 2010);
- a strong leader (Mascall & Leithwood, 2010; Fullan, 2010; Jensen, 2014a);
- distributed leadership (Fullan, 2010; Barnett & McCormick, 2012);
- well-behaved students (Hargreaves & Shirley, 2009; SSCEEWR, 2013);
- offering a wide selection of subjects and co-curricular activities (Hargreaves & Shirley, 2009); and
- a reputation of being innovative (Parsons & Harding, 2011).

I observed that a nearby secondary school, McAuley College (a pseudonym) had many of the above attributes. It also had enrolment waiting lists due to its reputation within the local community. The principal of the school, Jim Ford, was a colleague of mine and I had always been impressed by his passion and enthusiasm toward education. I was keen to learn how he had created the school's current positive culture and wanted to explore specific strategies that were used to cultivate this culture. Jim was enthusiastic about the proposed doctoral research being done at the school. This book explores one principal's approach to cultivating a positive school culture within the school community. The reader will gain a rich personal insight to how a highly effective principal can cultivate and maintain a positive school culture. It will also discuss the aspects that contribute to the cultivation of a positive school culture and the perceived challenges and benefits to the development of a positive culture within a school. The conclusive chapter will provide fourteen practical recommendations that leaders can implement to improve their own school culture.

1.2 Background

A well-performing school system is fundamental to building Australia's 'human capital' and is integral to the nation's economic and social futures. School personnel play a central role in promoting positive outcomes for students and the community generally (Productivity Commission, 2012). Schools are characterised by complexity, diversity and accountability measures which present significant challenges for school leaders. Principals, teachers and support staff all have an impact on student performance and there needs to be collaboration between the stakeholders if strategic policies and reforms are to be implemented successfully (Senate Standing Committee on Education, Employment and Workplace Relations (SSCEEWR), 2013). The key to the successful implementation of high school programs is school culture because this influences how teachers, school administrators and students behave and act (Rhodes, Douglas and Hemings, 2011). Principals play a crucial role in inspiring students, staff and members of the school community to continuously enhance the learning of all (Australian Institute for Teaching and School Leadership, 2011). Fredrickson (2009) reveals that the mood of leaders impacts upon the mood of the people they lead. This has significant implications for leaders as highlighted below:

> *Every action you do will either add to or detract from the culture of the school. It is the old emotional back account stuff. You are either adding to or taking away from the culture.* (Principal)

The Productivity Commission (2012) states:

Principals have primary responsibility for setting their school's culture. They and their leadership team provide the local foundation on which excellence in student outcomes are based.

Chapter 1: Introduction and Research Context

The role of the school principal continues to change and that school leaders today are required to display expertise in instruction, human resources, financial management, development, marketing, enrolment management and community relations (Nuzzi, Holter and Frabutt (2012). Researchers acknowledge the crucial role that the principal plays in cultivating a positive school culture within their own schools (Mascall & Leithwood, 2010; James & Connolly, 2009; Khalil, Kalim & Abiodullah 2013). Furthermore, Fullan (2005) notes that the principal is the key player in promoting change and sustaining the school's vision. A preliminary literature review established that:

- Leadership is an important factor of successful school outcomes and the culture of a school (Hargreaves & Shirley, 2009; Fullan, 2010; Mascall & Leithwood, 2010; Jensen, Hunter, Lambert & Clark, 2015; Edwards & Martin, 2016).
- School culture has a significant influence on the teaching and learning process (Fullan, 2005; Lima, 2006; Meredith, 2009; Ontario Ministry of Education, 2010).
- Culture has an important role in the performance of an organisation and without a positive culture, school improvement is difficult to achieve (Barth, 2002; Deal & Peterson, 2009; Parsons & Harding 2011).
- An important component of schools that have higher achievement results was each having a positive school culture (Fullan, 2005; Engels et al., 2008; Rhodes, Douglas & Hemings, 2011; Jensen, 2014b; Edwards & Martin, 2016).
- In order to improve the performance of students, principals need to make the establishment of a positive culture a high priority (Habegger, 2008; Holmes, 2009; O'Mahony, Barnett & Matthews, 2006; Rhodes et al., 2011).
- To establish a positive school culture, principals need to first examine the school's current culture (Keiser & Schulte 2009; Ontario Ministry of Education, 2010).
- Major cultural change is difficult to implement in a school and requires energy and commitment from all those who are implementing the change (Fullan, 2009; Sparks, 2009; Fullan 2010; Jensen, 2014b).
- School leaders hold extremely responsible positions that are complex, demanding, challenging and stressful (Bush, 2009; Khalil, Kalim & Abiodullah, 2013).

It is noted by Fullan (2009) that the development of a school culture may be very challenging for principals and it is claimed by some researchers that the cultivation of a positive school culture is the most essential task of a school principal (Holmes, 2009; Turan & Bektas, 2013). It follows that school leaders need to make the cultivation of a positive school culture a high priority since it impacts on school improvement and student achievement (Fullan, 2002; Engels et al., 2008).

The Australian Institute for Teaching and School Leadership (AITSL, 2011) acknowledges the crucial role of the school principal and suggests that in the 21st century this role is one of the most exciting to be undertaken by any person in our society. The school principal's impact is difficult to measure, however, few roles have more potential to shape society's future than the leader of a school. A recent study examining the Australian workforce in schools acknowledges their importance, and proposes that integral to the nation's economic and social future is a well-performing school system (Productivity Commission, 2012). The commission also recommends that school leaders be held accountable for their school's results as part of a rigorous performance management process. The key to the successful design and implementation of secondary-school programs is creating a positive school culture (Rhodes et al., 2011). Cleveland, Powell, Saddler and Tyler (2009, p. 51) state that, "School culture is a critical ingredient in the establishment of a successful learning environment." Current literature about school culture and leadership indicates that when school principals make cultivating a positive culture within their schools a high priority, there are significant benefits. These include:

> Culture is something that you need to be working on the whole time. It never gets to a point where it is stable, it in a constant state of change. It is not like you can have a holiday from it. (Principal)

- increased student motivation and achievement levels and teacher satisfaction (Harding, 2007);
- assistance in building and maintaining positive and caring relationships between staff, students and parents (Department of Education and Training, Queensland, 2014);
- promoting high staff well-being, commitment and affirming educational success (Rhodes et al., 2011);
- lessening the occurrence of school violence and bullying (Coyle, 2008);
- supporting the development of positive peer relationships as well as pupil engagement in learning (McGrath & Noble, 2010);
- encouraging other components of successful schools for continuous improvement to occur (Habeggar, 2008; Zbar, Kimber & Marshall, 2008); and
- assisting with school improvement (Habeggar, 2008; Zbar, Kimber & Marshall, 2008).

1.3 Purpose of the Book

My purpose of writing this book was to assist school communities, especially school leaders, to improve school performance by creating positive school environments that promote all aspects of student growth. This book combines current research in effective leadership and positive culture so that leaders are presented with the knowledge and practical advice to improve their results in their own school. Chapter 4 discusses the key behaviours of the principal that assist with the cultivation of a positive school culture. This section also provides practical recommendations which school leaders may apply in their own school setting. Every leader has a moral purpose to provide the best learning environment for the students in their care. This book is written so that principals can maximise the learning that is happening in their school. In doing so, they are creating a better future for the generations that follow. When examining their own school culture principals may like to use the Positive Culture Improvement Tool (Chapter 5) to apply many of the strategies presented. The strategies originate from the research site and give a rich insight into what the research school community believes cultivates a positive school culture.

> *There needs to be a shared moral purpose, which is doing what is in the best interest of our students.* (Principal)

1.4 Research Aims

The following information is derived from my thesis – Cultivating a positive school culture in a secondary school: The principal's role. The general aim of the research was to explore the role of the school principal in cultivating a positive school culture within the school community. Specific aims were as follows:

- to establish the aspects of a school community that contribute to a positive school culture;
- to describe the benefits of a positive school culture;
- to investigate what the challenges are for a school principal in the cultivation of a positive school culture;
- to explore the roles of the principal in establishing a positive school culture in the context of a leadership framework; and
- to document the recommendations of the school community for the cultivation of a positive school culture.

1.5 The Research Site and Context

Introduction

The first part of this section presents a broad overview of education in Australia and schooling in Queensland. A detailed description of the school where this research was undertaken is presented. Also, this chapter will explore some of the specific challenges faced by the school principal at the school where the research took place.

Overview of School Systems in Australian Schools

Introduction

In Australia, there are close to 10 000 schools. Approximately 67% are primary schools, 15% are secondary schools, 14% are primary and secondary schools and 4% are special-needs schools. Australia's education system is formed from several distinct, though overlapping systems. No other country in the Organisation for Economic Co-operation Development (OECD) has three different education systems – government, Catholic and independent (Gillespie, 2014). Approximately 70% of schools are state and territory government schools, 20% are Catholic schools and 10% are independent schools. Both primary and secondary schools are located in a wide range of settings whether that be in urban, rural or remote areas.

Government responsibilities for schooling

In the Australian context, schools are a state government's responsibility but are assisted financially through federal government funding. Recently this has caused much political debate as the various sides of government suggest pouring more money into education. Politicians need to tread carefully, as spending more money on education does not mean that students are going to achieve higher results. For instance, the state of Florida spent 20 billion dollars to reduce class sizes in its schools with little improvement, if any, on student achievement outcomes (Gillespie, 2014). Money must be spent on areas that make the biggest impact, such as improved leadership capabilities and teacher competences.

> Increasing educational funding does not equate to improved learning outcomes for students (White, 2015)

In Queensland, the government considers that education is central to Queensland's economic prosperity (Department of Education, Training and Employment (DETE), 2013). This view is acknowledged by the Senate Standing Committee on Education, Employment and Workplace Relations who add that the Australian government is implementing national educational reforms by providing funding for areas of national educational importance (Senate Standing Committee on Education, Employment and Workplace Relations, 2013). According to Caldwell (2015), the state government schools, as well as Catholic and independent schools, are dependent on the Australian government for much of their funding. Each state and territory government, however, has the responsibility of overseeing education within its jurisdiction. Responsibilities include: curriculum; infrastructure; governance and financial reporting. State and territory governments are also required to maintain a database of all registered teachers, and 'accredit' pre-service teacher education courses. In the past, there has been little policy coordination across the states and territories. Currently the Australian government is funding national reform initiatives, including the implementation of a new national-level policy framework, for Australian schools (Ministerial Council on Education, Employment, Training and Youth Affairs (MCEETYA), 2008). The success of the Australian government education initiatives is dependent on the cooperation of state government schools, independent schools and Catholic schools. The Australian government has made funding available to support these newly agreed-upon national initiatives.

The Queensland Department of Education and Training (2014) states that a high-quality education system is vital to the economic health of individual systems, states and countries. Furthermore, Australia's economic and social future is integrally linked to its school system and school staff play a central role in promoting positive outcomes for students and the community. The Senate Standing Committee on Education, Employment and Workplace Relations states:

Maximising our investment in our schools is of paramount importance to all Australians: the quality of education each student receives has important consequences for the student, his or her family and, ultimately, the Australian economy (2013, p. vii).

They further point out that Australian education policies are failing the lowest-performing students in Australia and these students are predominantly from disadvantaged backgrounds. The Productivity Commission (2012) argues that priority needs to be given to improving teacher quality, to reducing teacher shortages and to assisting the educationally disadvantaged. McKinsey and Company (2007) point out that "the quality of an education system cannot exceed the quality of its teachers" (p. 16). The AITSL (2012) believes that the ultimate goal of all teachers and school leaders is improving student outcomes and recommends that teachers need to embrace professional learning.

I think it is great when leaders continue to develop their teaching skills and understanding so they know exactly what the classroom teachers are doing and how they are doing it and they can have a conversation with the teachers. This allows them to be a leader of learning. An instructional leader. (Principal)

Furthermore, they assert that there is no higher priority than further improving the quality of teaching in Australian schools. In this respect, Edwards and Martin (2016) recommend that school leaders focus on building the school's culture to improve the performance of the school. This book explores how a school principal cultivated a positive school culture within their school community.

Goals of the Australian schooling system

The objectives of Australia's schooling system were articulated in 2008 in the Melbourne Declaration on Educational Goals for Young Australians. The two goals are: "Goal 1: Australian schooling needs to promote equity and excellence. Goal 2: All young Australians should become: Successful learners; confident and creative individuals and active and informed citizens" (MCEETYA, 2008, p. 7). The Melbourne Declaration sets the direction for Australian schooling for the next 10 years. This document aims for all young Australians to have access to high-quality schooling so that all students are given the opportunity to achieve.

The Case Study School

Type, location of school and demographic

McAuley College is a Catholic co-educational secondary school in regional Queensland. The school is the only school in Queensland that has only Years 7 to 10 (Year 7 was introduced in 2015). Some students travel over an hour by bus from surrounding areas. The school is located in the older area of the town and is surrounded by high-density dwelling and housing commission areas. In keeping with the Sisters of Mercy tradition of helping the poor and people in need, no family is turned away because they cannot pay the school fees. Fee discounts are readily given. The school is located in the largest sugar-producing region in Australia. It is also located in a regional town that services the mining industry in the Bowen Basin. Therefore, the financial health of the town is impacted on by the mining cycle of booms and downturns. After years of strong growth, the regional economy has recently suffered an economic downturn due to the low price of coal. In 2009 the school had no students who came from the top quarter income bracket across Australia and 52% of families were in the lowest income bracket. This changed significantly in 2015, when only 18% came from low income families.

Staffing and student enrolment

The school has a total staff of 89. This includes both full-time and part-time staff and those who are on leave from the college. The school's leadership team consists of the Principal, Deputy Principal, Assistant to the Principal Religious Education, Assistant to the Principal: Administration and Assistant to the Principal: Students. In the school, which is the subject of this research, there are 10 subject departments, each with a Head of Department. Other positions of leadership include four coordinators (Languages, Responsible Thinking Centre, Sport and History); six house coordinators; two other positions of responsibility (Guidance Counsellor and a Teacher-Librarian); 54 teaching staff and 35 support staff. Sixty-seven per cent of the staff are female. Approximately half of the school's workforce is under 40 years old. The current student population is 750. The school welcomes students from diverse cultural, social and economic backgrounds. The majority of students, 91%, are Australian citizens. Students come from diverse backgrounds including Maltese, Chinese, Vietnamese, Filipino, South Sea Islander, Aboriginal and Torres Strait Islander.

School's mission and vision

In 1968 the Sisters of Mercy opened the school and although there are no Sisters of Mercy teaching at the school today, the Mercy values are firmly entrenched in the school and the school's motto, "To serve Christ" which reflects the ideals of the school's founders. The school's vision statement is: "To serve Christ in humanity and grow in wisdom". The school's mission statement is – "We build foundations of optimism, faith, knowledge and creativity; we strive to achieve our greatest potential; we fashion a better world in keeping with God's plan."

The school principal is clear about the school's purpose:

"Our purpose is to deliver the highest quality of education in an environment moulded by Catholic values." Along with the vision and mission statements, the Mercy values of compassion, hope and justice are practised. The students regularly visit the elderly, help at St Vincent de Paul, read to young children at nearby primary schools, assist at Rotary functions and raise money for various charities. The school encourages relationships of respect and for students to act compassionately toward others in the community by practical service and giving.

> *The principal needs a clear vision for the future of the school, high expectations of staff and student achievement, (ensuring that all students are given the opportunity to learn to their full potential). (Parent)*

1.6 Education Issues and Challenges for School Principals

Introduction

The following section explores some of the specific challenges faced by the school principal at the research school.

Attracting and retaining quality teachers and leaders

Selecting capable and committed teachers is a core responsibility of a school principal (Marzano et al., 2005). Jensen (2010) states that the greatest resource in Australian schools is the teachers, as they have the greatest impact on student learning and adds that shortages are directly detrimental to the learning of students. According to Gillespie (2014), the two biggest drivers of improved student outcomes are the quality of teaching and leadership. The Productivity Commission (2012) believe that the success of education depends on the effectiveness of various reforms to attract high-quality teachers and help turn around the widely held perception that the status of teachers has declined. It recognises the need to improve teacher quality and reports that since the early 1980s, there has been a decline in the prior educational achievement of those entering the teaching profession. The AITSL (2011) also emphasises the importance of improving teacher quality and states that it is an essential reform to improve student attainment and to offer a world-class education system. The impact of quality teachers is felt long after lessons have finished.

> *The more upbeat, positive, happy and welcoming the principal, the more people will want to come to work and kids will want to come to school. (Teacher Aide 3)*

Distribution of workforce

Staffing all of Queensland's 1717 schools presents a unique challenge. The sheer vastness of the state makes it difficult to staff the small one-teacher remote school when most of the 57 000 teachers live in the more densely populated cities and regional towns, and are also reluctant to live in remote or rural communities (DETE, 2013). The Productivity Commission (2012) reports that the wide distribution of schools over a vast country is a major ongoing issue facing Australian education and the geographic distribution of the schools' workforce does not reflect the distribution of the student population. The lack of mobility of the workforce is hindering the staffing of regional and remote schools. The following statement from the school principal underscores his concerns about attracting staff to regional areas:

> What keeps me up at night is having quality staff so that I can harness their energy and point them in the right direction. This can be challenging in regional areas. (Principal)

Schools in rural and remote areas struggle to attract teachers and principals, and there is also a high turnover of staff in these schools. Furthermore, because of this, appointed staff often lack teaching experience and leave when they can get a position back in the city. This makes staffing of schools in these remote areas difficult even though there is a large surplus of teachers, particularly in the primary sector (Productivity Commission, 2012). In some secondary schools, the Productivity Commission (2012) found some significant subject-related teacher shortages and, as a result, teachers are often required to teach subjects in which they have no specialist knowledge or training.

A more complex and demanding teaching environment

Hargreaves and Fullan (2012) identify that there are many challenges facing teachers including: isolation; increasing expectations; contradictory demands; and feeling overloaded. To improve teaching, they recommend improving the working conditions that impact upon teachers – including the culture where they work. The Productivity Commission (2012) acknowledges that there are more demands and pressures placed on teachers and other school workers than in the past, and they warn that this is likely to increase in the future. The Productivity Commission (2012) gives the following reasons why school environments are becoming more complex and thus creating a demanding teaching environment:

- the demands on curriculum and pedagogy have expanded and become more complex;
- administrative load on teachers and principals has increased due to a greater amount of testing and reporting of student outcomes;
- parents and communities have higher expectations;
- schools are required to respond to an increasing range of social issues;
- the student population is more diverse;

- family structures are more diverse;
- there are concerns about the increasing incidence of inappropriate classroom behaviour; and
- an increasing number of special-needs students being taught in mainstream schools. (Productivity Commission, 2012, p. 6).

SSCEEWR (2013) recommends that teachers receive appropriate training to ensure they are equipped to manage student behaviour effectively. They also acknowledge that teaching is a complex task and recommend that both principals and parents support each other so that students are provided with an environment that is conducive to learning. They warn that high expectations of children's performance can be undone by poor behavioural management practices and poor student behaviour.

Leadership succession

In Australia, school authorities report a shortage of suitably qualified applicants for principal positions. Research conducted by the Australian Catholic University (CEL, 2004) reports that leadership succession is a major issue and is a looming crisis in school systems worldwide. While the quality of employed principals is high, the Productivity Commission (2012) warns that finding suitable

> *My worry is that too much depends on the principal. That is not a good principal, because it may be an ego trip if it does. That really worries me. The art and skill is ensuring the culture is resilient, and that the culture can bounce back no matter who leaves or what happens. So, you almost need to in some regards make yourself redundant or work toward making the culture that way. Therefore, you don't want to be too vital to the culture and hopefully you're not. You also don't want to be indispensable as this is a weakness. (Principal)*

replacements for principals is an increasing challenge. Duignan and Cannon (2011) also note that many schools are having trouble attracting suitable applicants for principal positions and add that there is a negative perception of the role, including the complexity and heavy workload associated with the position. They therefore believe that the principal's role is too multidimensional for one person and recommend that principals need to engage with others to support them in effectively leading the school. Jensen (2014a) also alludes to the problem that education systems need to develop their leaders and that the preparation in place for leadership is not good enough.

The schooling reform agenda

Historically, the responsibility for education lay with the state and territory governments. Recently, successive Queensland state governments have enacted education reform strategies, and the Federal Government, over the last decade, has become increasingly involved in education reform (DETE, 2013). According to Jensen (2014a), most educational reforms fail. He observes that nearly all programs that are introduced do not make a substantial impact. Caldwell and Spinks (2008) observe that increases in funding for schools does not equate to improved student results. SSCEEWR (2013) warns that improving school and student outcomes is not simply about spending more money; but that what matters is the way the money is spent and on what it is spent. Nicholas (2015) warns that governments around Australia have been spending money with little improvement and will not continue to do this. He states that Queensland is spending 1 in every 5 dollars on education and is reaching its spending limit. Fullan's (2010) research into successful reform proposes the following actions: have a small number of ambitious goals; guiding leadership; high standards and expectations; focus on instruction; utilising data to assist with improvement and intervention support. He adds that improving teacher and principal quality is at the centre of any system reform. Fullan (2010) recommends that whole systems need to focus on a small number of ambitious goals and will only be successful when the vast majority of people collectively work together to achieve them. A game changer will be when an educational system makes it a high priority to have a positive school culture in every school. Only then, I believe, will we see significant school improvement across all schools.

> *We can do more when we work together than when we work as individuals.* (Marzano, 2015).

1.7 Leadership framework

Overview of the ACGCEO Leadership Framework

There are a number of leadership frameworks for school leaders to assist school principals in their role. I reviewed various leadership frameworks to assist me with exploring the principal's role in my research. This section considers the leadership framework that has been developed by the Archdiocese of Canberra and Goulburn Catholic Education Office (ACGCEO). The framework describes the behaviour school principals are required to demonstrate in their critical role in building the capacity of their school community to provide a quality education. This framework was selected by me as it has been designed to assist in building effective leadership and to enhance individual school leader's capabilities to create high-performing learning communities. This framework provides strong links with this research in exploring the role of the school principal, in particular identifying the necessary skills, roles and behaviours of principals to successfully implement a school's vision and cultivate a school's culture. Furthermore, this framework provides an insight into what it means to be an effective school leader. This framework was developed to grow and enhance the skills required for effective leadership in schools and to enhance school principals' individual capabilities by listing specific behaviours that build effective leadership. To address the significant challenges, the ACGCEO (2009) state that school communities require exceptional leadership and have designed this leadership framework to provide a set of tools that will enhance the skills of leaders in schools.

Reflective questions

- What are some positive aspects of your present school culture?
- What would you like to change about your school culture?
- How can you continue to improve the quality of teaching at your school?
- What are the challenges facing your leadership?
- How are these similar/different to the challenges mentioned?
- How is your vision shared with the school community?

Decisive actions

- Examine the supporting behaviour in Table 1.2. Identify your top five biggest strengths and some behaviours you could improve.
- Examine the current school culture by asking the school community to complete the school surveys. (see Appendix A, B and C).
- Review your vision for the school. Explore how you can communicate it more effectively to multiple audiences.

Table 1.2 Leadership Capability Framework for Supporting Behaviours for Leadership in Catholic Education

Realm	Capabilities	Supporting Behaviours
Personal	Engages in ethical behaviour	• exemplifies honesty and integrity • demonstrates ethically responsible behaviour • is guided by the teachings of the Church
Personal	Is committed to personal and spiritual growth	• gives witness to personal faith and commitment • is self-reflective and emotionally mature • effectively balances work and personal life
Personal	Shows personal courage and resilience	• demonstrates confidence, optimism and resilience • is morally courageous • displays a sense of self-efficacy
Relational	Facilitates positive and collaborative relationships	• actively listens to the views of others • shares information and invites input from others • seeks mutually beneficial outcomes
Relational	Communicates skilfully	• communicates with influence • conveys messages and ideas with clarity
Relational	Inspires others	• recognises and responds pastorally to people • displays a trusting disposition • generates confidence in others to take action

Positive School Culture and Effective Leadership

Realm	Capabilities	Supporting Behaviours
Professional	Supports and builds Catholic identity and ethos	• operates with a spirit of service and professionalism • actively promotes Catholic values and traditions • manages conflict to restore positive relationships
Professional	Guides and mentors others	• nurtures leadership capability in others • provides professional support and guidance • affirms, praises and gives constructive feedback
Professional	Is committed to continuous improvement	• engages in learning and professional development • operates with a sound educational focus • acknowledges limitations and willingly accepts assistance from others
Organisational	Deals effectively with change	• develops organisational capacity to use new technologies to meet current and future needs • shapes and implements change processes • leads and supports others through change
Organisational	Delivers quality results	• focuses on core outcomes and accountabilities • models and encourages a strong achievement orientation in others • aligns actions with the Church's teaching
Organisational	Fosters a growth promoting workplace	• develops efficient and robust structures and systems • contributes to organisational sustainability • builds a culture that harnesses energies and talents
Strategic	Articulates vision and direction	• builds collegial purpose and vision for the school • interprets system and national strategic initiatives • gives priority to the Church's mission in education
Strategic	Thinks strategically	• uses 'big-picture' understanding to plan strategically • uses a variety of sources to make decisions • explores a range of solutions to deal with challenges
Strategic	Applies intelligence and wisdom	• reads and analyses situations accurately • applies logic and a common-sense approach • applies sound reasoning when taking action

(ACGCEO, 2009, p. 11)

1.8 Summary

In this chapter, the research context of the investigation was presented. A broad explanation of the Australian school system has been given and the objectives of this system were stated. One of the aims of Australia's education system is that every student should have access to high-quality schooling. The case-study school's vision and mission were explored and presented. The school was founded by the Sisters of Mercy and continues the tradition of the Sisters of Mercy of taking action in supporting others in need by being involved in community work. This chapter presented the ACGCEO (2009) leadership framework which listed specific behaviours and core capabilities that effective principals demonstrate in their leadership roles. Also, the reason why this framework was selected was also given. The chapter discussed some of the educational issues and challenges for school principals, including having a quality teacher in each classroom. Chapter 2 will explore strategies that school principals utilise to cultivate a positive school culture. Also, the next chapter will review the literature relevant to the leadership and positive school culture.

An excellent principal is a person who can lead a team of teachers to succeed, to feel they can excel and get the glory while part of a dynamic team. A person who can attend important events with big pompoms in the school colours! A person who can keep teenage boys interested in academic pursuits when they are 14 and essays do not excite them. A person who can exude joy and lead in tough times when the way forward is changing so quickly. (Parent)

A school principal should have strong expectations and enforce critical standards, while maintaining a positive and fair environment. Vision in all areas should be definable and should be shaped by relevant specialist advisers (HODs, Managers etc.). Good conflict resolution and public-speaking skills are also of key importance. (Teacher)

Chapter 2
Review of Literature When Exploring School Culture

Introduction

This chapter provides the current literature on culture and leadership. It will also examine the concept of positive school culture, define positive culture and explore the various influences that may impact upon school culture.

2.1 Defining School Culture

A review of the literature indicates that *school culture* is a broad term as there is no widely accepted definition of *school culture*. Most definitions refer to the rules, values and beliefs of a particular organisation and how these influence the behaviour and thinking of the people who are connected to that organisation. James and Connolly (2008) acknowledge that the difficulty of giving a simple definition of culture, as it is far too complex and is a problematic concept. This is because they believe that it is unclear whether culture resides in external factors away from individuals or within the minds and hearts of individuals. The beliefs and behaviour of the school community are of critical importance because these have a direct bearing on how people respond to challenges and how they interact with each other.

Deal and Peterson (2002) describe school culture as a complex pattern of norms, attitudes, beliefs, behaviours, values, ceremonies, traditions and myths that are deeply ingrained in the very core of the organisation. Similarly, Holmes' (2009, p. 5) definition describes culture as "A complex pattern of norms, attitudes, beliefs, behaviours, values, ceremonies, traditions, and myths that are deeply ingrained in the very core of the organisation." Fullan (2001) suggests that a school culture may be defined as the guiding beliefs and expectations evident in the way a school operates. Rhodes et al. (2011) believe that school culture is the key to successful design and implementation of school programs and this is the crux of the problem of educational innovation because it influences how members of a school community render into action educational practices. The beliefs and behaviour of the school community, according to these authors, are fundamentally of critical importance as they have a direct bearing on how people respond to challenges and how they interact with each other. Mohe (2008) found that organisational culture plays an important role in every individual firm and each firm has its own organisation culture. Dimmock and Walker (2005) add that organisations like schools are largely influenced by the society in which they exist and have distinct cultures that separate them from other organisations.

Rhodes et al. (2011) state that the core values of a school are the mooring blocks as to how people will interact with each other on a daily basis and that these are often on display in the staffroom to remind staff of what is important. Principals need to pay regular attention to how the school's core values are lived as they shape the culture of the school (Edwards & Martin, 2016). Taylor (2015) argues that culture is the manifestation of what is valued in the organisation. She expands further, stating that people observe these as messages and that they receive them from the behaviour, symbols and systems within the organisation. Pfeffer and Sutton (2000) claim that when core values are well understood, they can contribute to a company by providing a foundation of unified policies and assist people to decide what is important to focus on. These authors recommend that leaders model behaviours that they want others to implement. Therefore, it follows that leaders need to be held to the same standard as everyone else.

> People are watching him so he needs to model how he wants people to behave. (Parent 5)

School culture is built on the history and deep values of the school (Deal & Peterson, 2009). Schein (2004) refers to a pattern of shared basic assumptions which is taught to new members of the group as the correct way to perceive, think and feel in relation to solving problems. Meredith (2009) acknowledges the importance of how people feel about their workplace which impacts on their motivation and sense of belonging. Deal and Peterson (2009) stress the importance of culture by stating that it impacts on nearly everything that happens, including how people think feel and act.

Based on the foregoing, this research defines **culture as all the aspects that influence how a person thinks, feels and behaves within the organisation.** This definition acknowledges the complexity of school culture by recognising that there are many factors that influence how a teacher works and interacts with others. It is evident too that many of the school culture definitions neglect to mention that how a person thinks and feels will also shape their behaviour within that organisation.

> If they can see a positive leader, it all feeds down and it helps them to be positive. The positive culture is a reflection of the positive leader. (Parent 4)

Positive school culture

As this research is concerned with positive school culture, this section describes the nature of positive school culture as documented in the literature. Deal and Peterson (2002) define the term positive school culture as a culture found in schools that promote: shared leadership; student and teacher learning; collegiality; positive communication and respect for others. Collegiality can be described as the manner in which staff behave and interact with each other which assists in the creation of respectful relationships and Marzano et al. (2005) believe that collegiality supports staff to create relationships that are respectful, friendly and professional. They acknowledge that there is a positive relationship between school culture, leadership and overall effectiveness.

Chapter 2: Review of Literature When Exploring School Culture

A very powerful motivation is the relationship between the staff and the empathy and the environment that they create collectively. They can't tolerate being demeaned or devalued or embarrassed, but there needs to be a staff culture that has a high regard, warmth. They don't have to be best buddies, but the culture need to foster staff working together, sharing, and the staff need to go home happy. (Principal)

Fullan (2010) refers to collegiality as the social glue that enables people to work together. He observes that individual staff can thrive when immersed in a collective capacity mindset. When the individual and the group experience success, it compels each member to achieve more (Fullan, 2010). It follows that the building of a positive school culture should not be the sole responsibility of the leader, and Headsup (2014) holds that it is everyone's responsibility to create a positive working environment and that therefore everyone has a role to play in the establishment of a positive culture. The Ontario Ministry of Education (2010) recognises the importance of a positive school culture stating that a positive learning environment is the foundation of successful and high-performing schools.

Aspects of school culture

The literature reveals that there are many aspects that contribute to the formation of a school culture. Researchers use a variety of terms to describe what constitutes a positive culture including the following: characteristics; components; indicators; ingredients; domains; themes; features and elements. Deal and Peterson have listed what they consider as the core elements of culture: "a shared sense of purpose and vision; norms, values, beliefs and assumptions; rituals, traditions and ceremonies; history and stories; people and relationships and architecture, artefacts and symbols" (2002, p. 12).

According to these researchers, the school's values and vision statement can provide people with direction and a sense of purpose. They add that the values are at the core of what the school community views as important. In this respect, Harding (2007) asserts that an articulated mission statement, a clear understanding for excellence, commonly held values and vision are some common characteristics of organisations that display a positive culture. One of the first steps in cultivating a positive school culture is the promotion of a clear vision and core values for the school community to follow.

They need to catch the vision or the bus. You either want to be here or you don't. (Head of Department 2)

James and Connelly's (2008) research acknowledged that there are many influences that impact upon the culture of a school. Their findings concluded that the principal's leadership and reflective practices play an important role in shaping the culture of the school and the overall performance of the school they lead. Conclusions from a Belgian study (Engels et al., 2008), which compared principals in 46 different schools, found that schools that had positive cultures had shared values and a sense of purpose. Also, these schools were places where the development of relationships between members of the school community was viewed as important. These researchers found that the establishment of collaborative teams was given a high priority and there was an expectation of continuous learning and improvement for both staff and students.

Many aspects have been identified in the literature review that can contribute to a positive culture. Table 2.1 highlights the range of aspects that contribute to a positive school culture. Different schools may focus on various aspects of their own school culture and create a list of aspects or themes, such as the core values, behaviours and actions that are important to them (Alberta Education, 2005). Table 2.1 highlights the difference in opinions researchers and educational systems have regarding what constitutes a positive school culture. The above elements or indicators describe what a positive school culture may look like. Different schools may focus upon various aspects of their own school culture and create a list of elements or themes, such as the core values, behaviours and actions important to them (Alberta Education, 2005).

Table 2.1 Aspects of a Positive School Culture

Mission	Safe/Secure environment	Continuous learning
Purpose	Effective discipline	Curriculum
Norms	Equity/Fairness/Tolerance	Staff/Teachers
Values	Supportive strategies	Teaching/Learning
Beliefs	Behaviour management	Conflict resolution
Assumptions	Staff development/Roles	Symbols
History	Communication	Evaluation/Assessment
Stories	Collaboration	Trust
Relationships	Ethical standards	Students
People/Community	Empowerment	Caring/Respectful environment
Architecture	Support	High expectations
Artefacts/Physical environment	Events/Celebrations/Traditions	Perceptions/Thinking/Feeling
Excellence	Cooperative	Leadership
Collaborative teams	Rules	Purpose

The researcher's list of the aspects/themes that constitute a positive school culture was initially linked to Deal and Peterson's (2009) and Bustamante's (2009) research. This gave the researcher a guide to potential themes of focus for the data collection instruments (refer to Figure 2.1). The themes that were used to assist in the formation of the survey instrument for this research included: vision/mission/ values; curriculum; students; leadership; teaching and learning; building community; communication and conflict resolution; artefacts and physical environment; staff; and events/celebrations/traditions. The theme, *perceptions/thinking and feeling*, was included after a preliminary examination of the survey results. This was done when it became apparent how the school community thought and felt about the school and how this impacted upon their perceptions of the school culture.

Chapter 2: Review of Literature When Exploring School Culture

They can't just sit in an office, but need to walk around and teach a few grades. Principals need to show they value the students and staff. They need to be active in the school grounds. To build relationships they need to be caring, kind and compassionate. If they want their staff and the students to act in a certain way they must first model it themselves. So, if they set the example and build positive relationships, at the end of the day the results will be great. (Head of Department 1)

Figure 2.1 Themes of school culture for this research

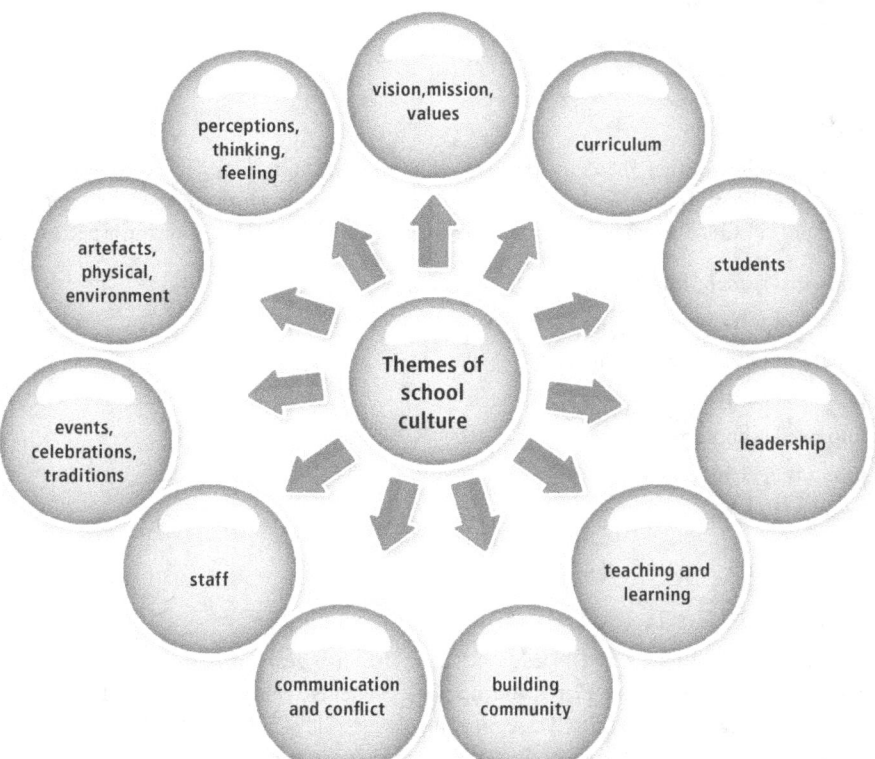

Reflective questions
- What are the behaviours you would like your leadership team to model?
- How do you create relationships that are respectful, friendly and professional?
- How does the school community know your school's values, goals and vision?
- What strategies can you implement that will improve the collaboration among staff?

Decisive actions
- Write down the key behaviours that the staff need to display to move the school forward.
- List the strategies you are going to implement that will encourage staff to display these actions.
- Create with your leadership team a small number of ambitious goals that will improve the capacity of staff to improve student learning.

2.2 Benefits of Cultivating a Positive Culture Within a School Setting

Introduction
The literature indicates that there are many benefits to cultivating a positive school culture and a synthesis of the literature has identified seven main aspects that are deemed to be beneficial to a positive school culture. The remainder of this section considers each of the following aspects separately:

- improved student learning;
- school improvement;
- enhanced positive relationships;
- increased motivation;
- improved school improvement;
- promoting change; and
- financial benefits.

Improved student learning
A major finding from Parsons and Harding (2011), after five years of research, found that schools that had high results are positive places and negative elements such as low morale had almost been extinguished. Brock and Groth's (2003) case study involving 50 low-income schools in the United States also found that their school culture was directly related to student achievement and was an important influence when implementing school change. This conclusion is also supported by other researchers who also state that positive school culture facilitates the enhancement of student achievement (Deal & Peterson, 2002; Tschannen-Moran & Gareis, 2004; Fullan, 2005; Jensen et al., 2015). Hargreaves and Fullan (2012) also note the importance of culture, stating that teaching is profoundly affected by the environment and workplace culture. They add that a school with a strong and positive culture has many

> *I think the positive culture basically maximises your outcomes for the students, otherwise so much of emotional responses are wasted in negativity and alienation. The energy needs to have a positive focus.* (Principal)

capable teachers, working passionately together and supporting the vision so all children can succeed. Research by Habegger (2008) examined four schools that were viewed as high achieving and concluded that the underlying reason why they were able to flourish and allow continuous improvement to take place was because these schools had a positive school culture. She also postulates that to improve the performance of students, principals need to give the establishment of a positive culture a high priority (Habegger, 2008). According to Engels et al. (2008) and Sergiovanni (2006) school culture has an important influence on student achievement.

Deal and Peterson (2009) supports Habegger's (2008) view and declares that the culture of the school plays a critical role in its performance. As mentioned previously, most reforms aimed at improving student performance fail (Fullan, 2010; Jensen, 2014b). However, various researchers conclude that without a positive culture school improvement is difficult to accomplish (Fullan, 2002; Fullan, 2010; Parsons & Harding, 2011). Various researchers repeat the importance of creating a positive culture to assist students to achieve higher educational outcomes (Helm, 2007; Habeggar, 2008; Holmes, 2009).

School improvement

A positive culture can assist schools with school improvement (O'Mahony et al., 2006). Cultivating and sustaining a positive school culture should be one of the highest priorities for all school principals because this is a crucial factor as to whether a school is successful or not (Engels et al., 2008; O'Mahony et al., 2006). Hattie (2015, p. 10) writes, "Not many schools promote what is actually most important for student progress: the quality of their teachers and school leaders." Hargreaves and Fullan (2012) concede that school reform and improvement have failed time and time again, often because the basic working conditions of teachers was not improved and this impacts on students learning.

Various researchers conclude that without a positive culture, school improvement is difficult to achieve (Barth, 2002; Fullan, 2002; Fullan, 2010; Parsons & Harding, 2011). The development of a positive school culture is therefore necessary for schools to turn low student achievement into higher student outcomes (Jensen, 2014a). O'Mahony et al.

> *Ultimately the teachers in the classrooms influence the students and motivate them to learn. Therefore, teachers have an enormous effect on the school culture.* (Principal)

(2006) send a clear warning when they declare that if principals choose to ignore the importance of their school's culture it will ultimately lead to failure. Therefore, the development of a positive culture is an important factor if school communities want to improve.

Enhanced positive relationships

Table 2.2 identified some of the benefits of a positive culture regarding positive relationships. Gray and Streshly (2010) contend that education is a human relations enterprise and therefore healthy human relations are a plus for any organisation. These authors also observe that when relationships improve, so does the school's performance. This notion is also supported by Hargreaves and Fullan (2012) who observe that groups, teams and communities are far more powerful than individuals. Turan and Bektas (2013) suggest that the individual aims of staff are more likely to turn into a shared objective in schools with a strong, participatory culture. They add that both short- and long-term objectives are reached more easily when a collaborative culture exists. Md Nor and Roslan (2009) also advocate for principals to develop a caring culture as it can promote positive relationships and a sense of belonging within members of the school community. Edwards and Martin (2016) encourage principals to model the school's core values to promote positive relationships and trust among staff members.

> *For staff, you get the best out of them. There is not much sick leave. Staff don't like to let people down so they want to come to work. For the students, they can see that we are happy to be there and it is a great place to be. They are safe, well looked after and are valued.* (Administration 2)

Increased motivation

According to Sergiovanni (2006) school cultures that are healthy have a high commitment from staff. It can be seen from Table 2.2 that some researchers like Mascall and Leithwood (2010) assert that positive school cultures correlate strongly with increased student motivation and achievement too. As a result, it can be seen that a positive culture that supports the growth and professional development of staff has the potential to improve student learning (Deal & Peterson, 2002; Bush, Briggs & Middlewood, 2006; Lima, 2006; Mutch & Collins, 2012). Khalil, Kalim and Abiodullah (2013) found that positive school cultures provide thriving platforms for students and staff toward excellence, and they also observed that schools that have negative cultures do not value professional development, resist change and devalue growth, all of which hinder success. Taylor (2015) observes that leaders should put time and effort into those things that they value highly. Hargreaves and Fullan (2012) recommend that teachers keep working to improve their teaching both individually and collectively to create high-performing teams. The notion that positive culture impacts upon school improvement is also supported by research from Canada, which found that students were more motivated to do well and achieve their full potential in schools that have a positive school culture (Ontario Ministry of Education, 2008).

> *Who would want to come to school if everything and everybody was negative? I think that the happier people are, the better they learn. You feel like you belong.* (Teacher Aide 3)

Improved school environment

As shown in Table 2.2, a positive culture can improve the school environment. Flaspohler, Elfstrom, Vanderzee, Sink and Birchmeier (2009) and Sadlier (2011) suggest that a benefit of having a positive school culture is that it contributes toward the reduction of bullying. Karakose (2008) contends that rules and values form the basic principles of school culture, which affects the emotions and thoughts of school staff. To reinforce cultural values, Pfeffer and Sutton (2000) recommend that an organisation's cultural values should be modelled and taught and learnt. A leader's principles are tested every day and they need to model and communicate what they view as important (Cosgrove, 2015).

Chapter 2: Review of Literature When Exploring School Culture

Mascall and Leithwood (2010) conclude that school leaders have a strong effect on school culture and classroom conditions, which ultimately impacts on the students' success, and Taylor (2015) believes that building a strong culture is the key to an organisation's performance; thus, culture is reinforced by people's behaviour. Therefore, leadership behaviour plays a crucial role on the building of culture because people look to the leaders for what is expected and important. Deal and Peterson's (2002) research into schools with negative cultures concluded that these schools lacked direction and purpose; blamed students for poor achievement; inhibited their enthusiasm; had little collaboration; had norms of behaviour that were negative and hostile; and were not healthy for staff.

Closely followed by enthusiasm, you need to have vitality and a zest for life. This needs to come through the leadership team. They need to be humble. They need to value others, and the dignity and worth of others, and be able to work with others. (Principal)

Promoting change

As shown in Table 2.2, a number of benefits in relation to promoting change are identified when there is a positive school culture. For example, Holmes' (2009) research examined the most effective practices by principals when creating school culture. Holmes concluded that principals needed to make the establishment of a positive culture the highest priority because all the members of the school community would then gain an understanding of these expectations, policies, procedures and values of the school. O'Mahony et al. (2006) hold that cultural change is made easier within a positive school culture environment. Harding (2007) also emphasises the importance of creating a positive school culture and claims that it is the principal's most important task. He adds that positive school culture influences every aspect of the educational program, including a school's ability to change and improve. Taylor (2015) argues that the purpose of cultivating the best culture is to create an environment that promotes behaviour that successfully achieves the organisation's goals. Holmes makes this important observation about culture, "What defines the culture will, in essence, define the school" (2009, p. 4). He expounds further on the importance of establishing a positive culture and claims that this is the driving force to a school's success.

Financial benefits

International accountancy firm, PricewaterhouseCoopers (2014), advocate for supportive workplaces as they believe they are good for business as they improve productivity, profitability, reduce staff turnover and lessen compensation claims. In his work as a coaching psychologist to business leaders, Sharp (2014) has identified the following benefits of building a positive culture: high levels of workplace satisfaction; high levels of engagement that contribute to productivity and ultimately to profitability; attracting the best people; keeping the best people; getting the most out of people and increasing collaboration and therefore better teamwork. Headsup (2014) also concludes that there are financial benefits to positive and supportive workplaces including: retaining staff and experience; improving

If you have a positive culture, we are all supporting each other. Your work production is going to be extremely high. (Administration 1)

productivity; lowering sick leave and encouraging staff loyalty. Taylor (2015) warns that poor culture has been the cause of behaviours that have cost companies large amounts of money and in some cases closed down organisations.

Reflective questions

- What has been your school's most successful reform in regard to improving student performance? Why did it succeed?
- What has been your school's least successful initiative? Why did it fail?
- How are positive relationships and trust among staff members promoted?
- How does the leadership team increase the motivation of your staff and students?
- What procedures or policies can you change that will increase the motivation of the staff and students?

Decisive actions

- Reduce the obstacles for staff and students to perform optimally.
- List ways you can improve the basic working conditions of teachers.
- Create a thank you wall. Staff can put up sticky notes acknowledging the supportive acts of others. Read these out at the start of each staff meeting.
- Discuss with the leadership team how to improve the quality of the teachers by developing a master plan.
- Have the difficult conversations with staff or students that address behaviours that are negative or hostile.
- Create a positive culture by trying to use more positive language and displaying acts of gratitude to staff.

Summary

Table 2.2 summarises aspects of the benefits of a positive culture. The benefits of each aspect have been provided, as documented in the literature.

> *Your staff wants to come to work then. They want to be there. The kids are happy. They put in extra work and everything works. Parents are happy and more things get done. People usually are willing to do a little bit extra or come up with ideas. People stop talking when it is negative. When it is positive you can do more things and people are more open to new ideas.* (Head of Department 1)

Table 2.2 Benefits of a Positive School Culture

Aspect	Benefits of a Positive School Culture	Author
Improved student learning	High-performance schools were able to flourish and continuous improvement occurred due to having a positive school culture.	Habegger (2008)
	Schools that have higher achievement results had a positive culture.	Engels et al. (2008) Sergiovanni (2006)
School improvement	Principals need to make a positive culture a priority.	Habegger (2008)
	Maintaining a positive school culture is important to improve student performance and school improvement.	O'Mahony et al. (2006)
	There are strong links with positive culture and increased student achievement and productivity.	O'Mahony et al. (2006)
	Employee performance and leadership effectiveness is influenced by the quality of the relationships.	Chen and Tjosvold (2005)
	Positive school culture is the driving force behind schools that are viewed as successful.	Holmes (2009)
Enhanced positive relationships	Education is a human relations enterprise. Healthy human relations are a plus for any organisation.	Gray and Streshly (2010)
	A safe, caring and inclusive school culture needs to be present to facilitate positive peer relationships.	McGrath and Noble (2010)
	When relationships improve the school gets better.	Gray and Streshly (2010)
Increased motivation	School cultures that were healthy had high commitment of staff.	Sergiovanni (2006)
	Leaders who are able to create cultures that embrace change can improve teachers' motivation/efficiency.	Deal and Peterson (2009)
	Positive school cultures correlate strongly with increased student motivation and achievement.	Mascall and Leithwood (2010)
Improved school environment	Having a positive school culture reduces the incidents of bullying.	Flaspohler et al. (2009); Sadlier (2011)
	Schools with positive cultures have high staff well-being.	Sergiovanni (2006)
	The rules and values form the basic principles of school culture, as the culture affects the emotions and thoughts of school staff.	Karakose (2008)
Promoting change	Make the establishment of a positive culture the highest priority because all the member of the school community will gain an understanding of expectations, policies, procedures and values of the school through acquisition of the school's culture.	Holmes (2009)
	Major cultural change is difficult to effect; however, it is made easier with a positive culture.	O'Mahony et al. (2006)
Financial benefits	Supportive workplace is good for business as it improves productivity, profitability, reduces staff turnover and lessens compensation claims.	PricewaterhouseCoopers (2014)
	There are financial benefits to businesses that provide supportive workplaces including: retaining staff and experience; improved productivity; lower sick leave and higher staff loyalty.	Headsup (2014)
	High levels of engagement, productivity and profitability; attract best people and keep them; and increased collaboration and better teamwork.	Sharp (2014)
	Culture impacts on performance and boosts growth.	Taylor (2015)

2.3 The Principal's Role and Practices in Cultivating a Positive School Culture

Introduction
As this research explores the principal's role and practices in developing a school's culture, it is appropriate to examine existing principals' practices and roles that cultivate a positive culture.

Role of the school principal
AITSL (2011) believe that the role of the principal of a school is one of the most exciting and significant undertaken by any person in our society. Principals work in an environment that is both complex and challenging; with each school being unique in that they have their own distinct ethos, culture, history, vision and values. A national standard has been developed to help define the role of the principal and this expresses three leadership requirements: vision and goals; knowledge and understanding; personal qualities, and social and interpersonal skills. Principals have a significant influence on the overall ethos of their school community that impacts upon the quality of education provided and, ultimately, the performance of students (Productivity Commission, 2012). The challenging complexity of their duties requires that the principal perform many roles (Bush, 2009). Duignan and Gurr (2007) also acknowledge that the job of principal includes many tensions and dilemmas and few other occupations match the job for complexity and responsibility. In many educational systems, schools are having difficulty attracting good quality applicants to the role (Duignan & Cannon 2011). Khalil, Kalim and Abiodullah (2013) surmise that recent research suggests that school leadership positions are viewed as being too demanding, stressful and lonely, and that they have unattractive pay structures.

> *The principal has a very important role. I kind of think if you have a negative principal that will have a flow-on effect. The more upbeat, positive, happy and welcoming the principal, the more people will want to come to work and kids will want to come to school.* (Teacher Aide 3)

Bates (2006) suggests that some of the complexities of schools originate from the cultural battles of the wider community being brought into the school by individuals or groups who voice their own particular points of view and interest. Duignan and Cannon (2011) and Siccone (2012) argue that we need to have a paradigm shift in how we view the role of the school principal, suggesting that the challenges and demands are too great for one individual and recommend that a distributed leadership approach is more appropriate. This is also supported by Hargreaves and Fullan (2012) who advocate for the development of a community of leaders who are able to work together to improve the performance of the school. Effective leaders are those that build the capacity of their school community to achieve the school's goals and articulate high expectations.

Principals are required to work in complex and challenging contexts which require them to collaborate with a wide range of people to secure the best possible learning outcomes (AITSL, 2011). Siccone

(2012) believes that there is no ideal leadership style that works best in all situations. He recommends that principals adapt to various leadership roles in response to the unique demands of their particular set of circumstances. Siccone (2012) makes the important point that the job of running a school is far too complex for any one person to do alone and the leadership needs to be shared. In a large high school the leadership team would share the responsibility of leading the school. O'Mahony et al. (2006) observe that in the strongest performing schools' leadership comes from many sources. The remainder of this section considers the various leadership roles that promote a positive school culture that have been addressed in the literature.

> *The principal has an administrative role. There is also setting the direction, the vision of the school. Setting the parameters for the school members. Making people know the boundaries. Building relationships and setting the tone for the school and valuing people is very important. I would like to give him a big rap for building a team that are willing to go that extra mile. (Parent 2)*

The principal's role as a school leader

Principals play a crucial role in developing the school culture and it is their leadership abilities and behaviour that are critical to maintaining and improving this culture (Lima, 2006; Meredith, 2009; Edwards & Martin, 2016). Holmes (2009) identified that there are other players in the creation of a positive school culture; however, the principal is the most important and influential individual in any school and plays a pivotal role in the production and maintenance of the culture of the school they lead (Rhodes et al., 2011). As shown in Table 2.3, various researchers stress this crucial role (Holmes, 2009; Bush 2009; Mascall & Leithwood, 2010; Siccone, 2012), and it is essential that they do this well (Engels et al., 2008). Principals influence and shape culture within their schools in ways that no other individual or external organisation can (Deal & Peterson, 2009). Edwards and Martin (2016) contend that principals are cultural builders and need to focus their attention on the culture of their schools.

Fullan (2010) observes that successful school systems have resolute leadership that is able to stay focused on achieving specific goals. O'Mahony et al. (2006) believe that principals influence the school's culture in everything they do; so, educational leadership is a vital component to school improvement because the quality of leadership makes a significant difference to school and student outcomes (Hallinger, 2003; Leithwood, Day, Sammons, Harris & Hopkins, 2006; Bush, 2009; Fullan, 2010; Siccone, 2012; Hattie, 2015). Leadership is strongly linked to academic achievement with Leithwood, Seashore Lewis, Anderson and Wahlstrom (2004), Siccone (2012) and Hattie (2015) claiming that this is second only to classroom instruction. Therefore, both good-quality teachers and effective school leaders are two key factors that contribute to improved student outcomes. Duignan and Cannon (2011) advocate for increasing the depth of leadership in schools by encouraging teachers to be involved in a shared leadership model so that they are actively involved in the decision-making of the school.

The principal's role as a relationship builder

Research from Scott (2003), investigating the most challenging aspects of being a school principal, concluded that principals were primarily concerned with relationships. Effective principals were able to deal with conflict situations and were able to work with people from diverse backgrounds and also contribute positively in group situations. Developing good working relationships with others is important, as the job requires much communication with a diverse range of people (Moore, 2009). Pfeffer and Sutton (2000) believe that the most important skill for leaders is the ability to work in teams and to collaborate with others. Therefore, a key skill for principals is their ability to reach a shared goal with stakeholders (Deal & Peterson, 2009). In order to create a positive school culture, Marzano, Waters & McNulty (2005, p. 157) recommend that principals should be aware of the teachers' needs in their professional and private lives, show teachers and students that they care and visit classrooms to establish close ties with all members of the school community. Edwards and Martin (2016) argue that having a caring and inclusive culture elevates schools from simply being good to being outstanding schools. As shown in Table 2.3, Devos and Bouckenooghe's (2009) research noted that all the schools with a strong culture had principals who were people-focused and who did not have an administrative-minded profile. The findings from this research suggest that there is a high correlation between schools with "strong climates" and principals who have a focus on people and educational matters, whereas weak climates tended to have principals who placed a high priority on administration.

> The things that make school positive for me are the teachers, my friends and the principal. If the principal is happy then the whole school usually is the same. (Student)

The principal's role as a visionary leader

Edwards and Martin (2016) observe that a school's vision can be the driving force in the life of a school and underlie every action and every decision within the school. Siccone (2012) recommends that principals articulate their vision with their school community as it enables them to lead with greater confidence, communicate with greater conviction and focus with greater precision. He expresses *leading with a vision* simply as, "Beliefs equal actions" (Siccone, 2012, p. 6). The school principal has to perform competently in a number of roles, including being a person who is a visionary and who can motivate and empower their staff (Engels et al., 2008). Stronge, Richard and Catano (2013) also emphasised the importance of the principal concentrating on a clear vision for their schools and never losing sight of the school's goals. A visionary leader articulates their own beliefs, values and assumptions clearly and often so that these are embedded in the organisation. It can be seen from Table 2.3 that an important role for the principal is setting direction and inspiring others (Davis, 2009). O'Mahony et al. (2006) observe that a feature of schools in which students were most likely to succeed are those that had a shared vision with the school community.

> I communicate these values every opportunity I get. I am conscious of that every time I speak in a public forum, whether that be a staff meeting or in a parent forum, school board speech night, it doesn't matter. You need to take a step forward and communicate these. I need to try and communicate principles that are going to help the school move forward at every opportunity. (Principal)

Chapter 2: Review of Literature When Exploring School Culture

The principal statement for school principals requires that school leaders develop a school vision based upon a clear moral purpose committed to the growth and development of the students (Catholic Education Diocese of Rockhampton, 2014). The leader's ideals and beliefs will be accepted and reinforced if they lead both the individual and the organisation to success (Schein, 2004; Siccone, 2012). According to Hoerr (2006) the leader of a school needs to articulate the vision of the organisation and focus upon building relationships and influencing school culture.

The principal's role as a change agent

Watkins (2005) commented upon the essential role principals play in a school improvement strategy or change initiative. It can be seen from Table 2.3 that principals hold a crucial position in any process of school change, as they are the most important and influential individuals in any school (Fullan, 2005; Hattie, 2015). Taylor (2015) holds that for change to happen leaders must also change. Sharp (2014) advocates for every single person playing a part in building a positive culture, because that way everyone can influence the culture of their workplace, regardless of their position. Habegger (2008) concluded that many of the roles principals play are important; however, none more so than building a positive school culture. Her findings support what has already been identified – that a positive school culture is imperative and that school culture is at the heart of improvement and growth. A noteworthy finding from her research was that the major difference between principals at the best-performing schools and those that were leading struggling schools was that the former group of principals focused on the need to create a positive school culture that promoted learning and engagement.

> *I believe a healthy dose of change can revitalise organisations and the people in them.* (Principal)

Sparks (2009) observes that a school's culture is difficult to change because people maintain beliefs and practices despite efforts to change them. Cosgrove (2015) states that leaders are accountable and responsible, and there is no higher duty than to inspire and make a difference to the children in their care. This may mean that school leaders are required to have some difficult conversations. Taylor (2015) believes that behaviour is primarily influenced by the environment. Therefore, by changing the environment, behaviour will change. She expands further stating that leaders need to take responsibility for their current culture because their behaviour, decisions and actions send messages to people on how they are to behave. However, Hargreaves and Shirley (2009) state that it is the teacher who is ultimately the arbiter of educational change because it is usually the teacher that implements the change in the classroom. Therefore, they recommend that teachers need to be actively involved in the whole change process and not just at the end. Duignan and Cannon (2011) argue for a paradigm shift away from how we have traditionally viewed principalship and recommend that leaders be more inclusive and collaborative to improve student learning.

Jensen (2014b) concedes that most reforms fail. He acknowledges that this is a huge challenge and recommends that students should be put first to enable improvement in teaching and learning. Fullan (2005) also acknowledges the difficulty of changing a school's culture. DuFour and DuFour (2007) believe that it is not because leaders have a lack of knowledge or understanding about the issues they face, but often because they do not implement the necessary steps to act upon the existing knowledge. This lack of action by school leaders is also noted by Reeves (2009) who believes that there is a widening gap between what school leaders know to be important and how they actually behave when they want to execute any changes. Therefore, it is leaders' implementation of new initiatives that is weak. Watkins (2005) holds that teachers have generally been excluded from having input into educational reform.

The principal's role as an instructional leader

Stronge et al. (2013) pronounce that nothing is more important for ensuring a high standard of student learning than effective instructional leadership. Coyle (2008) reveals that there is a relationship between instructional leadership and all the dimensions of school culture. It can also be seen from Table 2.3 that researchers believe that principals can play a significant role in teacher performance and student learning. Stone (2009) notes that principals who are instructional leaders empower others toward the goals of the school and encourage teachers to utilise best teaching practices, technological advances and strategies that promote high student achievement. Stronge et al. (2013) spoke of high-achieving schools having principals who had high expectations for all members of the school community and who held themselves accountable for the success of the school. Schools need principals with strong instructional leadership skills who can lead teaching and learning within their schools (Dinham, 2013).

The learning culture is important. The whole idea of staff embracing personal learning, along with students, needs to be embraced. You also need a structure that facilitates this. A culture that promotes learning is vital. (Principal)

Zbar, Marshall and Power (2007) and Caldwell and Harris (2008) assert that high-quality learning depends upon high-quality teaching. For principals to obtain the support of staff to achieve set goals, Kelley, Thornton and Daugherty (2005) suggest principals need to provide a satisfying place to work. Stone (2009) believes that these leaders advocate a team approach to school decision making which brings members of the school community to work toward school reforms and improvements. Fullan (2003) recommends that principals develop leadership skills in others so that the school leadership goes beyond themselves, and inspire members of the school community to improve their own skills by continuous learning. Fullan (2010) believes that instructional leadership has the most impact upon student performance compared with other styles of leadership. This is also supported by research from Sahin (2011) who found that instructional leadership has a statistically significant influence upon all factors of school culture. In this respect Edwards and Martin (2016) stress the importance of maintaining a positive school culture and state that a school's culture is directly linked to student achievement.

I know this is a cliché, but a leader of learning. I find there must be a need to busy themselves on what is happening in the classrooms and how kids are learning and encourage this and getting involved in it. Focusing upon the kids learning is the most important aspect of the role. And that is why principals should always need to have been good teachers first. This gives you credibility, which you need to have. (Principal)

Reflective questions
- What aspects of your leadership causes tensions and dilemmas? How are these resolved?
- What aspects of your leadership would you like to improve?
- How do you actively involve others in the decision-making of the school?
- How do you develop good working relationships with others?
- Are there some leadership tasks that you can share with other members of the school community?
- How do you articulate the vision to the school community?

Decisive actions
- Build the capacity of the leadership team and provide teachers with leadership opportunities.
- Delegate an administrative task that will provide you more time to visit the classrooms or meet with staff.
- Actively involve teachers with decision making in the whole change process.
- Explore ways that the administration personnel can improve their teamwork.
- Discuss with staff how to promote parent engagement so that parents are supportive of school rules, policies and staff.
- Explore with staff how they can communicate more effectively with parents.
- List ways that the school's vision and mission statements are lived in the corridors and classrooms by the staff and students.

Summary
The principal's behaviour has an influential role in shaping the culture of the school. Table 2.3 indicates that the principal is required to play many roles to meet the demands of the position. While all of the principal's roles in the school impact upon the school community, it would appear that none are more important than the shaping and building of a positive school culture. Principals who have a strong positive culture in their schools are able to articulate their vision to their community and motivate staff to utilise best teaching practices to improve the performance of the students. Furthermore, principals' leadership qualities do make a significant difference to school, and are strongly linked to student outcomes and can enhance cooperation between staff to actively promote learning for both students and staff members.

> They need to be a leader, a relationship builder, they need to ask lots of questions and really listen to the answers, so that they want to understand why something is not working or how we could do something better or even why something is working. Ask us if we are having any problems and ask what could be done better and take the feedback on board. I think they need to listen and then do something about it. That makes us then feel valued and supported and then we will want to do well because of the supportive environment that is present. (Head of Department)

> The principal displays a proactive role within the whole school and develops positive relationships with staff by engaging their strengths and appreciating their teaching skills through everyday communication and team building. (Teacher)

Table 2.3 Summary of the Key Principal Roles that Promote a Positive Culture

Aspect	Role of the Principal	Author
School leader	The principal's leadership abilities and behaviour are critical to improving a school's culture.	Mascall & Leithwood (2010)
	The quality of leadership displayed by the principal does make a significant difference to school performance and student outcomes.	Bush (2009); Siccone (2012)
	The principal sets the tone for the school and is instrumental if change happens in the school.	Holmes (2009)
	Principals need to lead by example to improve the school culture.	Sharp (2014); Gaster (2015)
Relationship builder	Principals are responsible for forging powerful relationships with the community they serve.	Midlock (2011)
	Schools with a strong climate have principals who were people focused.	Devos and Bouckenooghe (2009)
	Principals who were viewed as highly successful were experts in building relationships among members of their school community.	Gray and Streshly (2010)
	The principalship requires developing good working relationships with others.	Moore (2009)
Visionary leader	The role of the principal is about setting a direction and inspiring others to be part of the journey.	Davies (2009)
	All successful principals maintain a vision of improving student learning.	Gray and Streshly (2010)
	A visionary principal builds shared values and commitment to create a strong positive culture.	O'Mahony et al. (2006)
	Principals focus upon the core values and moral purpose to "promote and support the conditions for excellent teaching and learning."	Duignan and Cannon (2011, p. 27)

Chapter 2: Review of Literature When Exploring School Culture

Aspect	Role of the Principal	Author
Change agent	The role of the principal is to transform schools into professional learning communities.	Moore (2009)
	Principals must focus upon educational leadership as this is vital for school improvement.	Bush (2009); Siccone (2012)
	Principals assist staff to develop a shared understanding about the school's vision and goals.	Kouzes and Posner (2003); Fullan (2010)
	The moods, beliefs, values and attitude of the leader can influence the organisation's culture.	Fullan (2002); Holmes (2009)
	Cultural change is more likely to take place if leaders analyse the existing culture.	Fullan (2005)
	The most important person in any process of school change is the principal.	Hattie (2015)
Instructional Leader	The leadership of the principal is an important factor to improving student outcomes.	Siccone (2012)
	The principalship is strongly linked to achievement.	Gray and Streshly (2010)
	Principals who are instructional leaders empower teachers to learn.	Stone (2009)
	The main focus of the principal should be on teaching and learning.	Midlock (2011)
	Principals are the leading educational professionals in the school. They inspire the school community to learn.	AITSL (2011)

2.4 Strategies a Principal May Use to Promote a Positive School Culture

Introduction

This section considers seven strategies a principal may use to develop a positive culture within their school. The strategies were identified from a synthesis of the literature and the remainder of this section considers each strategy:

- audit of the school;
- establishing relationships;
- building community;
- articulating a shared vision;
- establishing a professional learning community;
- working toward collaboration/teamwork; and
- distributed leadership.

Audit of school culture

Just as a financial audit reveals strengths and gaps in financial procedures and practices to inform financial improvement, Bustamante (2009) recommends schools conduct a culture audit to inform how well a school is performing and to assist with school improvement planning. As shown in Table 2.4, an audit of the school can assist principals in gaining a deep understanding of their school. Deal and Peterson (2009) recommend that principals revisit the historical events or decisions that have shaped the school's culture. These authors claim

> *The principal needs to keep looking at how we can improve. Just because something worked once does not mean it will continue to work, next time it may not work at all. You can never be totally satisfied or happy with what is happening so you are continually searching for ways to improve the school.* (Head of Department 1)

that this will allow the principal to reinforce the positive things in the school culture and address the cultural aspects that are negative. Keiser and Schulte (2009) are strong advocates for evaluating the culture of the school in an intentional, thorough manner. To improve a school culture, principals need to first examine the school's current culture (Beaudoin & Taylor, 2004; Lima, 2006; O'Mahony et al., 2006; Keiser & Schulte, 2009; Ontario Ministry of Education, 2010). Beaudoin and Taylor (2004) claim that an audit of the culture will provide principals with a better understanding of existing attitudes, practices and issues within the community. Readers may like to use the staff survey in Appendices A, B and C to assist them in better understanding their school's culture.

Establishing relationships

Duignan and Gurr (2007) identified that a key theme that connected inspirational school leaders was their focus on valuing people and their appreciation of relationships as being a central part of their role. Table 2.4 highlights the importance of relationships in the

> *Our principal goes around through the classes and talks to the students and cares about what they have to say.* (Student)

development of a positive school culture. Fullan (2002) recommends that principals take the time to develop and nurture relationships because this assists in the development of a positive school culture. This recommendation also supports observations by Marzano, Waters and McNulty (2005) who suggest that in order to create a positive school culture, school principals need to show teachers and students that they care about them. This view is also supported by Rutledge, Cohen-Vogel, Osborne-Lampkin and Roberts (2015) who found that a positive school climate is created and student engagement is enhanced when teachers show concern for students' well-being and educational success. Parsons and Harding (2011, p.7) emphasised the importance of building relationships in schools and report, "Our research found that relationships are the key to every positive action within a school."

Chapter 2: Review of Literature When Exploring School Culture

Building community

A strategy for creating a positive school culture that is linked to establishing relationships is building a sense of community. Chiang's (2003) study examined the essential skills principals need to create positive school environments, and declared that effective principals are cultural builders. According to Hoerr (2006) effective leaders are ones that change people and since people are at the heart of organisations, it follows that simply changing people can create a positive culture, especially in schools. According to Md Nor and Roslan (2009) the principal plays a pivotal role in pursuing a sense of belonging among students. Similarly, Habegger (2008) observed that principals who had a positive culture in their schools gave a high priority to actions that assisted in building a community in their schools. Actions included: having clear directions and guidelines; a shared vision and belief that were a focal point; and an underlying team approach. Edwards and Martin (2016) warn principals against creating their own vision; instead they must consult with the school community to implement a shared vision for the school. Habegger (2008) found that one of the major activities of these principals was creating a sense of belonging through encouragement and treating staff as professionals so that they become successful in their roles.

Articulating a shared vision

If someone is doing a good job, tell them. Encouragement goes a long way. We need to hear the positives. (Administration 1)

Table 2.4 presents a summary of some strategies that a principal may use to promote a positive school culture, including articulating the school's vision. Raymer (2006) recommends that principals revisit and review the school mission statement with staff, as he believes this is a positive step toward developing and enhancing a school culture. An important observation made by Duignan and Gurr (2007) was that principals who were highly regarded by their community had clearly articulated their values and personal vision to their school community. This generated a deep moral purpose to their role. Moreover, leadership is associated with shared vision and ethical behaviour within the group (CEL, 2004).

Edwards and Martin (2016) observe that staff who have played a part in the creation of a shared vision are usually willing to commit to its achievement. Henderson and Thompson (2003) illustrate the importance of values on culture by describing values as the *DNA of an organisation's culture*. Lambert (2006) also recommends that principals need to hold fast to values if lasting school improvement is to occur. Sergiovanni (2006) states that organisations will be transformed from being ordinary to great if the values and goals that underpin the organisation are shared by the community for a common purpose, as the values guide behaviour and shape the way group members perceive, think and feel. Hargreaves and Fullan (2012) stress the importance of teamwork and observe that cohesive groups with less individual talent often outperform groups with high achievers because the latter do not work as a team. Pfeffer and Sutton's (2000) research of successful companies believes the success comes from the philosophy and values that the people embrace at the company. Deal and Peterson (1999) observe that everyone watches the leadership in the school and their behaviour plays a powerful role in shaping the culture of the school.

Establishing a professional learning culture

AITSL (2012) emphasises the importance of professional learning to improve student outcomes by assisting in changing teacher and school leader behaviour. To maximise student learning, Hattie (2015) asserts that school leaders need to ensure everyone works together toward improving student learning. Jensen et al. (2015) state that principals need exceptional leadership and management skills and need to keep up-to-date with knowledge about educational initiatives to lead improvements in teaching and learning. Zbar, Marshall and Power (2007) recommend that principals focus upon the greatest influence on student learning outcomes – the performance of the teacher. These researchers advocate for the building of a vibrant professional culture that supports high-quality teacher practice if student learning is to be positively influenced. This result is supported by Fullan (2010, p. 52) who simply states that *better instruction equals better results*. Hargreaves and Fullan (2012) advocate for whole systems to focus upon continuously improving every teacher and producing high-quality teachers in large numbers. It can be seen from Table 2.4 that establishing a professional learning culture can improve school performance. Stronge et al. (2013) advocate for principals to promote staff working together to take collective responsibility for the student learning. Duignan (2013) adds that a culture that promotes and supports strong core values and high ethical, professional standards is what is required.

> *He leads by example and talks about how we should do things and models what he expects. He is very approachable and his door is always open. He is always willing to listen and do what he can to help people in any way.* (Administration 2)

Working toward collaboration/teamwork

For schools to function there must be some degree of cooperation to exist. Harris and Jones (2015) remark that great sports teams, great businesses and great schools all used professional collaboration to raise performance. Fullan (2010) states that there cannot be successful reform unless the vast majority of people are working together toward the same goals. Pfeffer and Sutton (2000) recommend that leaders promote cooperation as this enhances organisational performance because there is a shared goal to which everyone commits. It is through the combined effort that each person's success is linked to the success of the organisation. According to Roffey (2007), there needs to be a connectedness between all the stakeholders if the organisation is to thrive. It can be seen from Table 2.4 that working toward collaboration and teamwork can improve the performance of schools (James & Connolly, 2008). Teachers need to be included in the decision to implement new initiatives because of the direct link between improvements in the quality of teaching and student performance (Hattie, 2009). Edwards and Martin (2016) observe that great schools have a culture of inclusion in the decision-making processes.

> *I like the teaching. I love the kids. I just love working with teenagers. They're great. The rapport you have with them allows them to learn so much. You have to have a rapport with kids. You have to enjoy kids – why would you be a teacher if you didn't?* (Head of Department 2)

McKinsey and Company (2007) and Fullan (2010) observe that the quality of an education system cannot exceed the quality of its teachers. According to Caldwell and Harris (2008) teachers have the greatest influence on student learning outside of the students' own ability levels. Collaboration is a vehicle that principals can use to facilitate teamwork and school improvement

> *First, they need a healthy understanding of what a collaborative culture is, including what is expected of them. Even though schools are made up of individuals the success and health of the school is ultimately decided by how individuals can work together.* (Principal)

as schools adapt to new situations. Hargreaves and Fullan (2012) recommend that principals promote collaborative cultures as teachers perform better when there is a collaborative culture characterised by a collective responsibility, dedication, places of hard work and staff pride in the school. Gaster (2015) supports Caldwell and Harris' (2008) views, suggesting that a collaborative approach to decision making assists with employees feeling valued and supported, which in turn facilitates motivation and performance.

Having distributed leadership

Stronge et al. (2013) believe that sharing leadership is indispensable to a school's success and contributes to sustainable improvements. They further point out that principals are able to utilise the expertise of the teachers to improve learning. Fullan (2003) suggests that school leadership should be viewed as a team sport and warns that you cannot have highly effective principals unless there is distributive leadership within the whole school. Jensen et al. (2015) hold that due to the increasing autonomy and accountability of the principal's role this has made the role more challenging due to the broadening of responsibilities. School leaders cannot do everything; therefore, principals need to develop the leadership skills of classroom teachers so there is a collective responsibility for the school (Watkins, 2005; Hargreaves & Shirley, 2009).

Staff involvement in the decision-making processes of the school can assist in building a positive culture where people feel valued, motivated and passionate about their work (Duignan, 2013). Watkins (2005) advocates for this development in teachers as he observes that ultimately it is the teacher that promotes school improvement in their classrooms. Hargreaves and Fullan (2012) note that the top-performing systems have a high priority in

> *A principal should be able to show great leadership, empathy and community spirit, and be able to challenge and encourage teachers and students to be the best they can be.* (Teacher)

developing their teachers. To improve the quality of teaching and learning outcomes, Duignan (2013) recommends educational leaders utilise the expertise and wisdom of their colleagues. He believes that when staff take responsibility for decision making, greater ownership and commitment to the implementation of new initiatives will be promoted.

Reflective questions
- What areas is the school performing well in? Where can the school improve?
- How do the staff know you care about them?
- How does the leadership team promote positive relationships among the school community?
- What are actions that create a sense of belonging among the students?
- How are you promoting a professional learning culture to improve student outcomes?
- How do you utilise the expertise of the teachers to improve learning?

Decisive actions
- Identify the strengths and weaknesses of your current culture by inviting members of your school community to complete the Positive School Culture Improvement Tool.
- Ensure the school's values and vision are clearly displayed around the school.
- Ensure that you are utilising the expertise of your staff by encouraging them to share this with students. This may include providing an extracurricular activity.
- Have the leadership team implement three strategies that will improve the teaching performance of staff.

Summary
From the review of literature, this section presented seven of the most common strategies principals can utilise to cultivate a positive culture and these have been summarised in Table 2.4.

Table 2.4 Summary of Principal Strategies to Promote a Positive Culture

Aspect	Principal Comment on Strategies	Author
Audit of school culture	It is critical that principals gain an understanding of existing practices.	Deal and Peterson (2009)
	Schools need to have an accurate picture of their existing school culture to confirm what is working well and where improvements are needed.	Ontario Ministry of Education (2010)
	An understanding of organisation culture is important for leaders trying to improve student outcomes.	Wagner (2006)
Establishing relationships	Principals need to establish relationships with all members of the community to build school culture.	Fullan (2002)
	Students who experience high-quality peer relationships at school are more likely to experience a range of positive outcomes.	McGrath and Noble (2010)
	School culture impacts upon the quality of relationships.	Wagner (2006)

Aspect	Principal Comment on Strategies	Author
Building community	Principals are required to be cultural builders and promote a culture that nurtures a sense of belonging.	Chiang (2003); Taylor (2015)
	Strong relationships built on respect between students and staff can also promote a sense of belonging.	Alberta Education (2008)
	Effective principals placed a priority on their teachers to develop positive relationships with students.	Habegger (2008)
Articulating a shared vision	The mission and vision statement is at the heart of a school's culture as it can motivate staff.	Raymer (2006)
	Principals need to be clear about their priorities and what they stand for.	Waldron and McLeskey (2010)
	Effective principals inspire others to see the vision of the school by living the vision themselves.	Kouzes and Posner (2003)
Establishing a professional learning culture	Professional learning communities provide teachers with the opportunity to address issues and collectively find shared solutions to improve overall performance.	Hargreaves and Shirley (2009)
	Principals need to be effective learning models by actively participating in professional development.	Stronge et al. (2013)
Working toward collaboration/ teamwork	For a school culture to develop and flourish, the principal's actions must model and support a collaborative culture in many ways.	Waldron and McLeskey (2010)
	Top-performing schools had high inclusive and collaborative cultures.	James and Connolly (2008)
Distributed leadership	To promote school improvement, principals need to use a distributed leadership model.	Fullan (2005)
	Sustaining school improvement demands principals develop their staff's leadership capacity.	Watkins (2005)

2.5 Summary and Conclusion

This section has presented an overview of the various definitions of school culture and explained the reasons for the definition selected. Most of the definitions refer to the rules, values and beliefs of a particular organisation and how these influence the behaviour and thinking of the people who are connected to that organisation. This review has also identified the many aspects that contribute to the formation of a school culture as seen in Table 2.1. It can be seen in Table 2.2 that from these aspects, the researcher formed themes in relation to a positive school culture and identified many aspects that contribute to this. The foregoing review of the principal's role in cultivating a positive school culture has identified some interesting conclusions from the research literature. Namely,

- there is a direct link to improving the school culture and greater student achievement;
- school culture is an important component in improving school performance as it can assist with effective implementation of new initiatives;
- developing a positive culture is highly desirable as it can influence many factors that contribute to student learning;

- the quality of leadership can make a difference to school performance and can be linked to student outcomes;
- the principal has an important role in shaping the culture of the school they lead, as they are the most important and influential individual in any school; and
- principals work in an environment that is both complex and challenging, with each school having aspects that are particular to them.

The review of the literature has revealed there are many aspects that contribute to a positive school culture. The literature does indicate that the principal is required to perform many roles to meet the demands of the job; however, none more important than building a positive school culture. The literature review suggests that there are many benefits for schools having positive cultures, these include:
- enhancement of the school's effectiveness and productivity;
- improvement in relationships;
- promotion of collaborative practices;
- fostering successful change and improvement initiatives;
- building on the commitment from all members of the school community; and
- increasing the motivation of students and staff.

In this chapter, the benefits of cultivating a positive school culture were considered and the reasons why it is important for principals to cultivate a positive culture were explored. The review revealed that the benefits of schools having positive cultures are that they:
- enhance the school's effectiveness and productivity;
- improve relationships and collaborative practices that foster better communication;
- foster successful change and improvement initiatives;
- build commitment from all members of the school community;
- increase the motivation of stakeholders;
- increase the focus on what is important and valued; and
- improve student learning.

They can't just sit in an office, but need to walk around and teach a few grades. Principals need to show they value the students and staff. They need to be active in the school grounds. To build relationships they need to be caring, kind and compassionate. If they want their staff and the students to act in a certain way they must first model it themselves. So, if they set the example and build positive relationships, at the end of the day the results will be great. (Head of Department 1)

Our principal makes a point of coming into the staff room at break time and actively engages in conversation with all staff. By building a relationship with each and every staff member they feel comfortable coming to see him if a problem does arise. (Teacher)

Chapter 3

Discussion of Results

3.1 Introduction

This chapter specifically discusses the results of the research with respect to each of the research questions. Due to the hundreds of pages of results, only a portion of the quotes were included to maximise the readability of this book. This chapter will also discuss the links between the behaviours of effective leadership listed in the ACGCEO (2009) leadership framework and the behaviour demonstrated by the school principal in the research.

Research Question 1

RQ 1 – *What aspects of a school and school community contribute to a positive school culture?*

Research Question 2

RQ 2 – *What are the perceived challenges for the school principal in cultivating a positive school culture?*

Research Question 3

RQ 3 – *What are the perceived benefits of a positive school culture as identified by the school community?*

Research Question 4

RQ 4 – *What are the roles of the principal in establishing a positive school culture?*

Research Question 5

RQ 5 – *What are the recommendations from the school community for the cultivation of a positive school culture?*

Research Question 6

RQ 6 – *What are the characteristics or behaviours of an excellent school principal?*

3.2 What Aspects of a School and School Community Contribute to a Positive School Culture?

Introduction

The following 14 key aspects that contribute to a positive school culture emerged from the research results. Many of these aspects also have strong links to the recommended behaviour of effective principals that are listed in the ACGCEO (2009) leadership framework:

- treating each other respectfully;
- having a friendly school community;
- the presence of positive relationships between members of the school community;
- school's values and vision are known to all;
- having high expectations of each other;
- students displaying good behaviour;
- principal having a positive and enthusiastic attitude;
- the need for an engaging curriculum;
- students having a sense of belonging;
- aesthetics of the school are of a high standard;
- principal models the behaviour he wants others to display;
- the school environment is safe and caring;
- staff work collectively to achieve school's goals; and
- high job satisfaction by staff.

The remainder of this section considers each of these aspects.

Treating each other respectfully

The research findings showed that respectful relationships are strong indicators of a positive school culture. This result was evidenced by the comments from staff and parents about being able to identify if a school has a positive culture

> *The core values are very much about respect. Respect for yourself and others.* (Parent 8)

by the way people treat each other. The values being taught at the school were viewed by the parents as an important aspect that contributed to the quality of education that was being offered. Both the students and parents suggested the most important virtue that is promoted by the school is respect, as

Chapter 3: Discussion of Results

highlighted. This result is consistent with that reported by Deal and Peterson (2009) who suggest that a school's success is largely influenced by the relationships that exist between members of the school community. According to these researchers a culture can be shaped by the leader's daily interactions with other members of the school community. Staff mentioned the importance of wanting to be at the school. In this research, the principal believed that trust among the staff was an important element of a school's culture. This finding supports the work of Hargreaves and Fullan (2012) who note that groups that are built upon trust and have purpose learn more and perform better. The principal placed a high priority on building positive relationships built on trust and respect. An important action by the principal was that he showed that he cares and respects the students. The principal placed high importance on student well-being and positive staff/student relationships.

This result is in accord with the ACGCEO (2009) leadership framework that acknowledges the importance of relationships between staff and students, and states that high-performing leaders respect others and are respected by them. This was also evidenced by the comments of the students themselves, who reported that they are treated with respect by staff, and is similarly reported in the research literature. For example, research suggests the importance of respectful relationships in regard to overall effectiveness of school performance (Marzano, Waters & McNulty, 2005; Engels et al., 2008; Fullan, 2010; Hargreaves & Fullan, 2012).

> *When staff feel that they are treated with respect and are trusted that will transfer to the kids. You can therefore expect that those processes are going to treat the staff and kids well.* (Principal)

Having a friendly school community

Staff believe that you can tell if a school is positive as soon as you come onsite. Some staff mentioned that besides the principal, the people working in the front office have a significant influence on school culture and give a strong impression to visitors about the culture of a school. The principal stressed the importance of the front office staff being warm and friendly, especially with the initial greeting. This finding is supported by Hargreaves and Fullan (2012) who note that this culture shapes the experience you have as soon as you walk into a school and that an indication of a positive culture is that office staff are friendly and courteous. The staff survey results confirm *friendliness* as a common response, as well as *positive attitudes* which can enhance the learning environment. Comments from the students indicated that a school that has a positive culture is a place where people would want to come. In this respect, the principal is required to seek mutually beneficial outcomes to enhance the work environment.

The presence of positive relationships between members of the school community

Staff spoke about the principal's ability in building positive relationships with the staff. These findings are in accord with Meredith (2009), who contends that the principal needs to develop positive relationships with all employees in order to cultivate a positive school culture. The ACGCEO (2009) leadership framework suggests that principals are required to inspire others to respond positively and to motivate them to work together as a team. A high priority for the principal was the cultivation of positive relationships between members of the school community. This result is consistent with that

As you walk into a school you can tell if it has a positive culture by how you are treated and received. If people are smiling and enthusiastic and are happy in what they are doing, they are glad to be there. You can tell by the way people treat each other. (Administrator 2)

of Noonan (2004) who suggests that there is a common thread to creating a positive school culture, namely, the importance of relationships. He argues that students' ability to develop supportive relationships is as essential a skill as learning mathematics and how to read. The results indicated that staff were treated with respect, felt valued by the leadership team, and that they also had positive relationships with the students. This accords with the findings of Holmes (2009), who contends that effective leaders build relationships within their school community.

The comments from the focus groups and interviews highlighted the importance of relationships when cultivating a positive school culture. Relationships reduces friction between people and acts as a lubricant to all the various aspects that form a culture, so that actions can happen more effectively.

Following up, the research is clear on this: the kids' outcomes improve when you have parental involvement. We are using every opportunity to say that parents are welcome here and to come along. (Principal)

School's values and vision are known to all

The principal indicated the importance of communicating the school's values and expectations. He communicated the school values and vision to the school community often. This finding is supported by Kouzes and Posner (2003) who reveal that effective principals inspire others to see the vision of the school by living the vision themselves. Edwards and Martin (2016) also support this finding and state that successful principals keep a shared vision a focus of their leadership. This school's vision was guided by the Mercy Sisters charity, reflected in the importance the school placed upon respectful relationships and serving others. The results highlight the importance parents placed on the school values. They not only wanted the students to achieve success academically but also wanted values to be explicitly taught. It appears that the underlying school values influences how community members interact with each other. This result is consistent with Pfeffer and Sutton (2000), who observe that organisations that have strong cultures operate according to a set of principles and values that are consistently implemented. They add that precedent is the "glue" that holds these firms' behaviours together and it is these shared values and beliefs that shape actions more so than formal bureaucratic procedures. Rhodes et al. (2011, p. 83) state in their research that values influences people's behaviour for how everyday life in offices, classrooms and corridors is actually lived and are vital for the success of all educational initiatives.

An important message from the staff to the students was the need for them to look after each other and the idea that service is a core value of the school. Rhodes et al. (2011) report similar findings in regard to the impact of values, which form the foundation of the school's organisational culture because they have a profound influence on how people behave. The importance placed on the promotion of school values, as stated in Chapter 2, has been similarly observed in research by Keiser and Schulte (2009) who found that schools which display the shared values of fairness, justice, respect, cooperation and compassion have a positive sense of community that supports and motivates both teachers and students.

Maintaining high expectations of each other by the principal and school staff

The principal would often remind the staff at meetings of his expectations and model these and the school's values. This outcome aligns with the ACGCEO (2009) leadership framework which asserts that principals need to consistently ensure work from themselves and others is of a superior standard. Parent responses indicated that the principal has high expectations of staff and students' behaviour. When discussing

> *I was going to say ... expecting and supporting high expectations. Part of that is by example. Part of that is he expects good teaching, he expects good behaviour from children. (Parent 1)*

the question, 'What is the most important role of the school principal?' The parents highlighted the importance of the principal maintaining high expectations. This research has confirmed that the principal daily sets the tone and expectations of the school and how people are to behave. This finding supports Gurr's (2015) research on how school leadership influences student learning, and he found that successful principals consistently maintained high expectations which focused upon helping individuals to achieve their best. The results from the survey indicate that the teachers do encourage students to do their best and how they treat the students does impact upon the motivation of the students and their learning.

Students displaying good behaviour

Almost all members of the school community felt that the students were well behaved. The school implemented an effective behaviour management program. A key reason for the effectiveness of the program was that it was consistently applied by all staff. Analysis of the responses from the survey has identified that the behaviour of the children is regarded as a strong characteristic of the school as reflected by the following survey comments:

> *Generally great student behaviour. (Staff)*
>
> *High standards of expected behaviours are asked of students. (Parent)*

Aspects of a positive school culture identified by staff are: respectful interactions; following of school rules; and students displaying good behaviour. Staff also recommended the need for students not only to learn academically but to also develop virtues like compassion and empathy. A caring environment and effective behaviour management were also indicated by staff to be important aspects of a positive culture.

The staff also reported that when students were well behaved, this was conducive to teaching and creating a positive learning environment. This result confirms Rhodes' et al. (2011) observation of the importance of having an effective student behaviour management policy that includes clearly stated codes of conduct that promotes core values.

> *I love teaching my subject and love my kids going into senior. I love to see past students I taught go on to achieve. This warms my heart. I come into work for my students. My students are awesome.* (Head of Department 1)

Principal having a positive and enthusiastic attitude

The survey results overwhelmingly showed that the school community viewed the principal as enthusiastic and positive. This result is in accord with the ACGCEO (2009) leadership framework which recommends that principals always operate from a positive viewpoint and have a positive and confident approach to leadership. A finding from this research is that principals need to be positive themselves if they want to cultivate a positive culture within their schools. This finding aligns with Sharp's (2014) recommendations which state that if leaders want happy employees then they need to be happy themselves. The principal was seen as supportive by his presence at all school events. The parents liked how the principal was both visible and approachable. The students commented upon his classroom visits and taking the time to talk to them in the playground. They saw the principal as friendly and supportive. The school community identified the key role of the principal in shaping the school's culture. This research finding also demonstrates the alignment with the literature findings, for example (Lima, 2006; O'Mahony et. al., 2006; Meredith, 2009; Mascall & Leithwood, 2010; Parsons & Harding, 2011) identified that the principal plays an important role in the cultivation of a positive school culture.

> *Staff are willing to go that extra mile and they have been great and exceed the expectations, and this comes from the principal. The principal models this himself. Staff are willing to do these extra things. The team they have there is very strong and the staff all over-deliver in their support of the kids.* (Parent 1)

Chapter 3: Discussion of Results

The need to have an engaging curriculum

The principal suggested in the interview that it was important for the school to offer outstanding programs and signature programs so that each child has an opportunity to achieve success in some area of the curriculum. Also, the teachers need to provide a variety of high-quality curriculum programs that give all students the opportunity to achieve success and develop a sense of belonging. It is difficult to teach a child who does not feel they belong (Marzano, 2015). The principal indicated that it was important for the school to provide opportunities for the students to achieve success and gain a sense of belonging and states:

> *A co-curriculum program that essentially gives every kid a chance to succeed and have a sense of belonging. It is not about winning. It is about the kids finding a niche that they like and caters for their social needs, which promotes them being the best that they can be. That is the enduring goal. (Principal)*

The staff acknowledged that the school offered a wide selection of subjects as reflected in the following comment from the staff survey:

> *Our extra-curricular options are amazing. Staff are always engaging with students trying to make their time at school more enjoyable. (Staff)*

The large number of extra-curricular opportunities and the subject options were identified by the student respondents. A finding from the survey data was that the extra-curricular opportunities and wide subject selections were viewed very favourably by the parent and student community. The parents indicated that the values that the school promoted were important. In the school survey the students indicated that the extra-curricular activities and wide variety of subjects were positive aspects of their school.

The staff clearly felt that the school is providing enough extra-curricular activities and the variety of subject selection appealed to both the students and parents. Also, students indicated that some subjects are enjoyed more than others because of the teacher. A large majority of the school community believe that all students are expected to achieve success. The implementation of a new curriculum brought with it some challenges, with some staff stating that it has added to the workload of teachers. Aspects that contribute to a positive culture include: students are expected to achieve; effort and achievement is recognised; there is a wide selection of subjects; students gain a sense of belonging; students are encouraged to participate in a variety of extra-curricular activities; and the curriculum provides all children with the opportunity to succeed. The results show that the principal advocates for students to be given a choice of subjects and that it is important that the school offers a diverse set of programs so that each child is given the opportunity to achieve success and gain a sense of belonging.

Students having a sense of belonging

The ACGCEO (2009) leadership framework indicates that accomplished principals are highly influential in unifying commitment to the common purpose and enthusiastically motivating others. Positive social interaction was viewed as an important element of a positive school culture. The staff believe that positive affirmations, positive language and the house system all contribute to developing the students' sense of belonging. The students suggested that the principal made them feel welcomed by greeting them and visiting classrooms. Developing friendships was regarded as a very important aspect of school culture by the school community.

> He makes everyone feel special and good. He makes you feel confident when he talks to you and congratulates you. I feel valued when he talks to me. (Year 8 Student)

The importance of students developing friendships is evidenced in the principal's following commentary when he talks about the importance of students belonging to the school community:

> We have house coordinators and they are expected to get on the front foot and be proactive in regard to activities and events for the kids, pastoral care and giving the kids a sense of belonging. (Principal)

The parents reported that there were a number of things about the school that they or their child liked. The most common responses were in regard to their child having positive relationships with their peers and their teachers. The focus group research indicated that making friends was very important for the students and, likewise, having the opportunity to mix with their friends was valued by the students. The following statement from a student indicates the importance the students placed upon friendships:

> It is a lot like a place where you can go and make friends, because without friends you don't get anywhere. It is not always about the work. (Student 7)

The importance of students having a sense of belonging is supported in the research literature. For instance, Habeggar (2008) found principals that had high community connections created a positive school culture by engaging in activities such as: visiting each teacher before school started; creating a sense of belonging by greeting students; building relationships; and encouraging staff to have positive relationships with the children they teach. The results from this research and that of the Ontario Ministry of Education (2010) recognise that feelings of belonging can enhance students' self-esteem and can contribute both to improvements in academic performance and behaviour.

Aesthetics of the school are of a high standard

Results from the principal's interview indicate the importance of the physical environment as an indicator of school culture. The principal believed that first impressions count and made the aesthetics of the school a high priority. The presentation of the grounds was a strong indicator of a positive school culture and the staff appreciated working in a school that was so well presented.

Chapter 3: Discussion of Results

> *I think the whole physical environment as you enter the school is important. The little things, the tiny things, like objects that are in disrepair, but try not to be too flash. Good to have kids work up, the fish tank. Our art teacher always displays the kids' artwork in the front foyer, which looks good. They get greeted in a very short space of time. The initial greeting is very important.* (Principal)

The parents in the interviews suggested that the physical environment is an important aspect of a positive school culture. The religious symbolism around the school had a significant influence as it maintains the school's identity. The importance of symbolism was mentioned by all groups, with the principal and staff stating that it reminds the school community of what is important. This supports the findings of Taylor (2015) who states that symbols and rituals are effective ways of bringing a community together.

Principal models the behaviour they want others to display

The data revealed cultivating and maintaining a positive culture was a major focus for the principal and he felt that school principals were indispensable in the cultivation of a positive culture. The results from this research show clearly that the principal's behaviour influences other members of the school community and this finding is supported by the research literature, in which O'Mahony et al. (2006) emphasise that principals communicate their core values every day and reinforce these to the school community in their words and by their actions. The principal was aware of the important influence of leadership behaviour in shaping others in the school community.

This finding is aligned with Cleveland et al. (2009) who observe that effective leaders model the leadership they want others to emulate. With regards to leadership actions purported by Sadlier (2011), a leader's core beliefs are exposed and expressed through the way in which they engage in their conversations and actions. The results from the parent and staff focus groups and interviews suggest that how a leader acts has a greater influence on the culture of a school than their words.

> *So, there are many benefits and you know that the kids are going to be treated well. If the teachers aren't treated well, they won't understand that they must model this expectation of treating the kids in a positive manner, including the language they use. This must permeate to the kids. The respect levels must be evident when teachers interact with the kids. When staff feel that they are treated with respect and are trusted that will transfer to the kids.* (Principal)

The school environment is safe and caring

The school community believed that the school provided a very caring and safe environment. The Safe Schools Action Team (2008) believes that a safe and supportive environment for learning is one of the most important factors that influence student learning and performance. The results from the principal's interview showed the importance he placed upon respectful relationships between the staff and students which is aligned with research from Hargreaves and Fullan (2012), who warn that when social capital is weak, everything is destined for failure. In this respect, the Ontario Ministry of Education (2010) acknowledges that all students require a caring and safe environment in order to learn and develop their potential. Similarly, Hargreaves and Fullan (2012) emphasise the importance of schools providing a positive culture as this impacts on everything that happens in schools. The survey data reveals that teachers play a significant role in how their students feel about the school.

> *I think he/she would have to have a positive outlook. They need to at meetings instil that positivity into people even when things are going on. They need to lead by example.* (Head of Department 2)

> *When I have a good teacher, I am happy to go to their class. Even if the subject is not a strong one for me, the teacher helps me and is really friendly.* (Year 10 Student)

Staff work collectively to achieve school goals

The principal was able to unite the staff to work together to achieve the school's goals. This was clearly demonstrated by the amount of extra-curricular activities that the school was able to offer. There was an expectation that every staff member would provide extra service so that the school could provide a rich and engaging curriculum. The school community perceived this aspect of the school as a significant strength. The principal relied on a distributed leadership model to ensure that staff had some input in decisions. Heads of Departments were expected to support staff in their department. There were also clear guidelines and procedures in place so that staff knew what was expected of them. The school also provided shared planning time so that staff had opportunities to plan together. There were regular meetings so that staff had a good understanding of what was happening.

High job satisfaction by staff

The results indicate that the staff experienced a high level of job satisfaction. The staff in the focus groups and interviews made many comments about the enjoyment they received when working with the students and being part of the school. Findings from this research indicate that a positive school culture encourages both the staff and students to come to school. This aligns with the research literature indicating that workplaces that have positive cultures have workers with higher levels of job satisfaction and productivity (Sharp, 2014; Headsup, 2014).

> *Sometimes I go into the classrooms and have a bloody ball. Recently I came back from the music trip out west and I said to them, I don't think I should have got paid, I thoroughly enjoyed myself. Our role is a privilege.* (Principal)

This section provides a summary of the school community's response to each research question. The above discussion has demonstrated alignment between the literature and findings of this research.

Chapter 3: Discussion of Results

The principal needs to have good communication and lead by example. An excellent principal should have an understanding of the needs and wants of his students and the pressures they may face. An excellent school principal is one that can have fun and enjoy his/her work. (Parent)

Reflective questions
- How do you support student and staff well-being?
- What impression do visitors receive about the culture of a school when they visit the front office? How can this be improved?
- How do you motivate staff to work together as a team?
- How do you promote the school values?
- In what ways do you encourage staff to consistently maintain high expectations?
- What are the most rewarding aspects of your role?

Decisive actions
- Chapter 3 identified 14 key aspects that contribute to a positive school culture. List in order the aspects you need to give the highest priority.
- Review the Positive School Culture Improvement Tool and find ten ways that you can build positive relationships with your school community.
- Walk around the school with an architect or landscape designer and explore ways the aesthetics of the school could be enhanced.
- Each day, take some time off administrative tasks to visit some classrooms.
- Discuss with staff the importance of maintaining high expectations and explore with them. What are the behaviours that as a staff they need to demonstrate?
- Provide a surprise lunch or organise a coffee van as a sign of your gratitude and an acknowledgement of the staffs' commitment (especially at report writing time!)

Summary of Research Question 1

There were some commonalities between the groups to what they considered were aspects of the school that contribute to a positive school culture. Many of the behaviours of effective school principals listed in the ACGCEO (2009) leadership framework contribute to the cultivation of a positive school culture including: builds collegial purpose and vision for the school; models and encourages a strong achievement orientation in others; operates with a sound educational focus; and engages in learning and professional development.

The staff and students suggested that there would be high expectations. Students displaying good behaviour were identified by all three groups. The staff and parents mentioned the importance of values. All three groups indicated well-maintained grounds were another aspect that contribute to a positive school culture. The promotion of friendships was stated by the parents and students. A sense of belonging was identified by the staff and students as an aspect of a positive school culture. The importance of respect was often mentioned in the research results.

Table 3.1 School Community's Response to Research Question 1

RQ 1 What aspects of school and school community contribute to a positive school culture?		
Principal and staff	**Students**	**Parents**
• people speaking to each other respectfully; • high job satisfaction; • vision and values are evident; • aesthetics of the school; • positive learning environment; • positive relationships; • collaboration and distributed leadership; • students displaying good behaviour; • a sense of belonging; and • high expectations.	• good student behaviour; • a caring environment; • friendships are encouraged; • sense of belonging; • well-maintained gardens and grounds; • having high expectations; • getting along with others; • friendly and caring place; • students displaying good behaviour; and • extra-curricular activities.	• underlying values; • friendships are encouraged; • students getting along with others; • grounds visually appealing; • development of virtues; • the promotion of a learning culture; • positive social interaction between staff and students; • students are encouraged to do their best; and • happy staff and students.

3.3 Discussion of Research Question 2

What are the perceived challenges for the school principal in cultivating a positive school culture?

Introduction

The research literature in Chapter 2 indicates that a principal is faced with many challenges in cultivating a positive school culture. The results from the research identified the following key challenges:

- maintaining a positive school culture;
- the school community working collaboratively toward the school's vision and goals;
- attracting and retaining high-quality staff;
- developing teachers as leaders;
- promoting change;
- assisting staff in a demanding teaching environment;
- developing positive relationships between all members of the community; and
- improving student learning.

Maintaining a positive school culture

The principal is faced with many challenges when trying to cultivate a positive school culture. A finding from the principal's interview was that they must continually work on creating and maintaining a positive culture, and this emerged as a challenge for the principal. The principal recommended that school leaders keep trying to cultivate a positive culture and it is something that leaders need to be working on the whole time. The principal holds that leaders are always influencing culture through their actions and communication. This aspect of the principal's leadership was an obvious strength as the results revealed that the principal had excellent communication skills and this was an aspect of his principalship that he did exceedingly well. The moods, beliefs, values and attitude of the leader can influence all levels of the organisation; this includes its culture (Fullan, 2002; Schein, 2004; Holmes, 2009). Edwards and Martin (2016) recommend that principals take time to maintain a positive culture.

The school community working collaboratively toward the school's vision and goals

The ACGCEO (2009) leadership framework describes a supporting behaviour of effective principals as *building collegial purpose and vision for the school*, and therefore principals are required to clearly articulate the school's mission. The results from this research found that the principal needs to continually be active in the team-building processes. This result confirms other research about the role of the principal by Schein (2004) who states that culture is a dynamic phenomenon that surrounds people and is being constantly enacted and recreated by our interactions with others, and shaped by leadership behaviour. The principal, staff and parents indicated that keeping the school community supporting the vision of the school was a challenge. The AITSL (2011) observed that when school leaders work in partnership with parents there is a greater commitment from the school community to achieving the goals and vision of the school. A similar finding was reported by Alvy and Robbins (2005), who recommended principals articulate the school's goals and vision often. Pfeffer and Sutton (2000) found that even companies often underestimate the importance of the underlying philosophy that guides what they do and why they do it.

Attracting and retaining high-quality staff

The principal was able to describe some of the major challenges that impacted upon his school, including the establishment of a positive culture and attracting quality staff. This aspect of his leadership aligns with the behaviour of effective principals from the leadership framework (ACGCEO, 2009), which recommends principals be aware of the challenges and plan strategically to address these. The principal stressed the importance of attracting good-quality staff to offer a high-quality education.

The results in this research are aligned with the broad consensus within educational research that indicates that teacher quality is the single most important in-school factor influencing student achievement (OECD, 2005). This result is supported by many educational researchers, including Hattie (2009), who concludes that the effectiveness of teaching has a significant effect on student learning outcomes. The availability of attracting quality staff is also recognised by the Productivity Commission (2012) who expressed the following concern, "On the shortage side of the ledger, there are some significant subject-related teacher shortages at the secondary school level. As a consequence,

Staffing is another major concern I would have. Attracting good quality staff is necessary to offer a high-quality education. (Principal)

teachers are often required to teach subjects in which they have no specialist knowledge or training" (2012, p. 65). Furthermore, Stutz (2015) states that schools located in regional and remote settings have always faced difficulties such as access to resources compared to schools in cities.

Developing teachers as leaders

The ACGCEO (2009) framework states that effective leadership is critical to the success of any organisation and a core capability is that principals guide and mentor others. This includes the effective delegation of tasks to others and providing professional support to maximise the performance of all staff members. The principal's ability to utilise the expertise of his staff and further develop their skills to achieve the school's goals was an obvious strength. The principal expressed a concern that the culture should not be dependent on one person and recommends that school leaders develop the capacity for their staff to lead. This result is similar to Fullan's (2010) findings who warn about cultures being too reliant on one person. During his interview, the principal advocated for a distributed leadership model. He relied on his leadership team to support him in achieving the school's goals and suggests that school leaders continually regard team-building as a priority. This strategy is supported by Jensen (2014b) who recommends that school leaders direct their energies into improving their teachers. The principal also encouraged staff to seek professional development opportunities and this supports the work of Edward and Martin (2016) who promote the need for principals to utilise the skills of all members of the school community to improve school results. Better trained teachers raise their capacity to produce higher outcomes.

Promoting change

Table 1.2 states that a supporting behaviour of highly competent principals is shaping the change process by supporting others through the changes. The results in this research indicate that promoting change is another challenge for school principals. The principal observed that the culture is never stable and that it is always in a state of change. He adds that principals cannot take a holiday from cultivating a positive school culture due to schools being in a constant state of change and, importantly, Hargreaves and Shirley (2009) advocate for teachers be actively involved in the proposed changes if they are to be successfully implemented. Cultivating a positive culture creates an environment that motivates people to try things that they have not done before.

Assisting staff in a demanding teaching environment

The principal recommended that leaders implement appropriate procedures and systems to promote school growth. By developing efficient and robust structures and systems principals are better placed to support their staff in a complex work environment. The parents raised a number of concerns about the principal trying to meet everyone's expectations and satisfy their needs. The staff conveyed concerns about the negativity of some staff and that it would be a challenge when staff are not positive and supportive. Parents also expressed concern about how to handle negative parents and that addressing unsupportive and negative behaviour from people was a challenge for school leaders. Administration staff made mention of the busyness of the role of the principalship and also that the principal has to deal with so many issues.

> *I don't think people really appreciate the technical expertise that goes with teaching a diverse range of students.* (Principal)

Developing positive relationships between all members of the school community

In this research, managing relationships successfully was viewed as another important challenge for principals. This result is also aligned to assertions made by the Education Review Office (2008) who found that leadership is crucial in creating meaningful and respectful partnerships. Staff and parents suggested that it would be difficult for the principal to treat everyone fairly while at the same time trying to meet everyone's needs. This result indicates that developing positive relationships with all members of the school community is a significant challenge for a school principal. The ACGCEO (2009) leadership framework indicates a core capability for all school principals is the ability to promote positive and collaborative relationships among the school community. They add that principals are required to have a consultative approach and value the contribution of others.

Corsbie (2014) recommends investing in relationships to improve students' outcomes. The principal made time each day to leave his office and talk to the students and staff. This observation is aligned with the recommendations of Edwards and Martin (2016), who believe that principals need to make time to have personal conversations with every staff member to improve collaboration and relationships.

> *For me a positive school culture has an attitude or an aura within the school, that you see people that are keen to be there. Staff want to be there, kids want to be there. Everyone interacts in a positive way, or a happy way or a productive way. You don't have that negative feeling and you can feel it. You can walk into a school and feel that it is a positive school.* (Head of Department 2)

Improving student learning

The results indicated that the principal placed a high priority on both the staff and student learning to promote school improvement and a positive school culture. The findings from this research support the recommendations from the leadership framework (ACGCEO, 2009) that principals be committed to continuous improvement. Improving student learning was identified as another key challenge identified by the school community. Both the parents and students suggested that creating a positive learning environment would be a challenge for the school principal. This was also acknowledged by the principal in his interview when he stressed that it was important that school leaders make learning a high priority in order to improve student learning. Synthesising the available research evidence, Masters (2007)

The academic achievement is very solid. There is a strong learning culture. We need to keep providing quality teachers. There is a culture in this school that kids are expected to learn. And teachers are expected to try. That doesn't happen in all schools. (Principal)

concluded that highly effective teachers are those who *create classroom environments where all students are expected to learn successfully and they strive for continuous improvement.*

Reflective questions

- What are some of the major challenges that are impacting on your leadership?
- How are you developing your teachers as leaders?
- How do you promote change?
- How do you ensure everyone is treated fairly and respectfully?
- How do you support staff to be committed to continuous improvement?

Decisive actions

- List ways you address unsupportive or negative behaviour from people.
- Review the Positive School Culture Improvement Tool and list ways you can improve relationships with students.
- Explore ways staff can have more time to plan together to implement the curriculum more effectively.
- Share a coffee with a trusted colleague and discuss with them what is keeping you up at night.

Summary of Research Question 2

Khalil, Kalim and Abiodullah (2013) contend that professional development has now become crucial for educational improvement. The school community was able to identify many challenges for the school principal in cultivating a positive school culture. There were a number of behaviours of effective principals from the leadership framework (ACGCEO, 2009) that matched the responses in Table 4.2, including: builds a sharing organisational culture that harnesses energies and talents; develops a culture of continuous learning; consistently displays and articulates the values and vision of the school; influences and manage change effectively; and facilitates positive and collaborative relationships.

All groups mention that ensuring all people were supporting the school's vision was a challenge. The creation of a positive learning environment/culture was also mentioned by all three groups. The parents and staff suggested building positive relationships was viewed as a challenge. Students and parents thought that having all staff appropriately trained in all subject areas was another challenge for the school principal. The staff and parents commented on the difficulty of trying to support all the needs of staff, with the students adding that making everyone happy and safe would be difficult. Dealing with negative staff or parents was also seen as a challenge by the parents. Creating and maintaining a positive school culture was also mentioned by staff and parents as a challenge.

Table 4.2 School Community's Response to Research Question 2

RQ 2 What are the perceived challenges for the school principal in cultivating a positive school culture?		
Principal and staff	**Students**	**Parents**
• maintaining a positive culture; • attracting quality staff and then retaining staff; • improving student learning; • having staff supporting the school's goals and vision; • continual team building; • managing change; • supporting so many staff; • having positive relationships with all people; and • continuous focus on school improvement.	• being responsible for everyone; • making everyone happy and safe; • ensuring all teachers are suitable trained; • trying to get all people supporting the school's vision and policies; • ensuring everyone follows the school rules and expectations; • attending many events; and • creating a positive learning environment.	• challenging embedded practices that currently exist; • having appropriately trained staff in all subject areas; • meeting the needs of all staff; • attending all the activities; • the promotion of a learning culture; • people supporting the vision and rules; • building positive relationships with all staff; and • dealing with negative parents.

3.4 Discussion of Research Question 3

What are the benefits of cultivating a positive school culture?

Introduction

The results in this research indicate that there are many benefits to cultivating a positive school culture, including the following:

- students and staff are more motivated to learn;
- obtains high student academic achievement;
- increase in the level of collaboration between members of the school community;
- promotes positive relationships;
- both staff and students want to be at the school;
- creating a more positive workplace;
- improving student behaviour; and
- leaders having a positive focus.

Students and staff are more motivated to learn

Staff made comments about the benefits of a positive school culture including: improvement in student performance, behaviour, motivation and enjoyment. The research by Deal and Peterson (2009) also found that a positive school culture increases staff and students' motivation and commitment. The principal believed that having a positive school culture motivated the staff to improve their own performance and achieve better results. He suggested that student behaviour issues lessened, and this created a more positive learning environment. This finding supports Gillespie's (2014) view that behaviour management is critical to effective learning. Poor student behaviour increases when teachers are not supported by the school principal (SSCEEWR, 2013, p. 10). Safe School Action Team (2008) found that students are more motivated to achieve their full potential in schools that have a positive school culture.

> *Academically I think we do better if we have a positive school culture. We do better and get better results out of our students.* (Head of Department 3)

Obtaining high student academic achievement

The results from both the focus group sessions and interviews demonstrated that staff, parents and students believe that a positive school promotes academic achievement. This result confirms previous research by Keiser and Schulte (2009) which argues that creating a positive school climate is essential for increasing academic performance, enhancing social and emotional skills, and even retaining staff. According to Leithwood, Harris and Strauss (2010), strong leadership that raises expectations is vital for schools that want to lift student performance. Meredith (2009) observes that as the school culture becomes negative it has a detrimental effect on relationships and student achievement. The above result supports the findings by Keiser and Schulte (2009), who found that developing a positive school community improves academic performance, and this is in accordance with Khalil, Kalim and Abiodullah (2013) who report that the school culture plays a decisive role and impacts the overall performance of a school's success or its failure.

Increasing the level of collaboration between members of the school community

Staff observed that when working in an environment with a positive culture staff support each other and their productivity is higher. This finding supports Hargreaves and Fullan's (2012) research which suggests that it is better as a teacher to be collaborative than individualistic. The staff indicated that there is greater collaboration and support when there is a positive school culture, and Hargreaves and Fullan (2012) report that teachers learn and improve more when they are able to work with others. Fullan (2010) observes that staff in

> *We have been working on that recently. Following up the research is clear on this: the kids' outcomes improve when you have parental involvement. We are using every opportunity to say that parents are welcome here and to come along.* (Principal)

Chapter 3: Discussion of Results

successful districts in Ontario are effective due to their willingness to work collaboratively. Hattie (2009) observes that collaboration between staff assists with change as teachers develop new or improved approaches. Also, collaboration can have a powerful effect in magnifying and spreading the benefits of professional learning (AITSL, 2011).

Both staff and students want to be at the school

A finding from the individual interviews was that staff are attracted to positive workplaces. This finding concurs with Pfeffer and Sutton (2000) who recommend that employers create positive work environments if they want to attract and retain staff. Staff in this research also felt valued and appreciated. This result is consistent with Taylor's (2015) findings that people thrive on receiving some form of recognition and that people are more likely to improve their performance if they feel valued because their positive motivation is stronger. Mother Teresa made a thought-provoking quote for all leaders to action, *"We cannot do great things, you can only do small things with great love."*

A finding from this research is that a positive workplace encourages people to want to come to work and be willing to give more and engage with others. The results reveal that a positive environment makes learning more enjoyable, improves overall performance and makes students happier. The findings

I really enjoy my job, I love it. I love the interaction with the other staff and the students. I enjoy all aspects. (Teacher Aide 2)

from this research support the observations made by Waters (2009) that connectedness to school is positively linked to student mental health outcomes, which is fostered through the culture of the school.

Creating a more positive workplace

The results presented in Chapter 3 suggest that staff are happier in a positive workplace. A similar result was reported by Fullan (2010) who suggests that improved working conditions assists all teachers to be quality performers. Staff suggested that people take ownership of what happens to them and this promotes leadership and learning. Hargreaves and Shirley (2009) suggest that Finland has high retention rates because teachers are given status, support, small classes and autonomy. A teacher expressed that a benefit to them was that it reduced stress. In this respect, reducing stress can improve performance as teams that operate in stressful environments are less collaborative and more likely to make mistakes (Business in the Community, 2009). Staff suggested that people do not want to work in a negative environment, but rather in a positive place. The principal made it a habit to thank his staff often. He felt it was important that staff know that their contribution matters. This result also was confirmed in research by Guin (2004) who found that the schools that lacked a positive culture had the highest rates of new teachers leaving the teaching profession.

Friendly, warm, welcoming and appreciative. I just love all that. The people here are great. Students are just well mannered. It comes from the top. (Teacher Aide 1)

Improving student behaviour

Staff attribute improvement in student behaviour to having a positive school culture where students want to go to class and learn. The results from the online survey show that 99% of the respondents agreed that students at the school are well behaved. Responses from the students indicate that there would be less bullying and that people are happier, more helpful and treat each other better when there is a positive school culture. These

> When staff feels that they are treated with respect and are trusted that will transfer to the kids. You can therefore expect that those processes are going to treat the staff and kids well. (Principal)

findings are aligned with Rutledge's et al. (2015) research which states that the higher-performing schools had effective behaviour management systems that addressed students' academic, social and emotional needs. They also suggest that schools which promoted student engagement, high expectations of student behaviour and had positive school cultures also had fewer disciplinary infractions. Hargreaves and Shirley (2009) acknowledge that one student with extreme behaviour difficulties can disrupt a whole class and have a significant negative impact on the class results.

Promoting positive relationships

The results show that the staff have positive relationships with their students and a positive attitude toward teaching. A high priority for the principal was the pastoral care of the students and this ensured that the students have a sense of belonging. The positive culture assisted the principal to have open and trusting relationships with his staff. This finding supports Meredith's (2009) research that an important role for principals is to develop positive relationships with all employees. In this research, another significant benefit that the principal attributes to a positive school culture is that the students are going to be treated well. The results also indicate that students had positive relationships with their teachers. This may also be one of the reasons why bullying was rarely mentioned by the students in this research. Students who are bullied, and those who bully others, report feeling uncared for by their teachers (Sourander, Klomek, Ikonen, Lindroos, Luntamo, Koskelainen & Helenius, 2010). They believe that promoting a positive classroom environment, and positive relationships between students and their teachers, assists in the reduction of all forms of bullying.

> If they want their staff and the students to act in a certain way they must first model it themselves. So, if they set the example and build positive relationships, at the end of the day the results will be great. (Head of Department 1)

Leaders having a positive focus

The principal recommends that school communities have a positive focus and was a strong advocate for school leaders cultivating a positive school culture within their own schools because of the positive benefits. The results for the research participants revealed that there is an identifiable link between improved performance and cultivating a positive school culture. In concluding his thoughts on his role, the principal summed it up by declaring that a principal's job is to be effective. This confirms the following reflection concerning school improvement by Fullan (2010, p. 63) who states, "It is only what works that counts." The results from this research indicate that a positive culture allows the leadership team to have more open communication. The principal believes in professional dialogue with his staff as he was actively involved in what was happening in the classrooms and this result is also supported by Taylor (2015) who recommended that leaders articulate their expectations. Meredith (2009) suggests that effective leaders are measured by the successes of the people around them and therefore need to empower others to take an active role in their organisation.

> To be unfailingly positive. Being affirming and positive is important. I quote, "to be slow in my aggravation, but lavish in my praise that is the secret". This is important, as is support. (Principal)

Reflective questions
- How does a positive school culture enhance academic achievement?
- Why is it better as a teacher to be collaborative than individualistic?
- How can the school attract and retain quality staff?
- How do teachers create positive relationships with their students?

Decisive actions
- Discuss with staff how they can create a more positive learning environment in their classrooms.
- Examine the behaviour management program. Explore ways it can be more consistently applied.
- Discuss with staff how they can contribute to creating a positive workplace.
- Explore ways the school can engage parents more effectively.
- Each day, try and search for the good in the school community. Acknowledge publicly the behaviour you want to see and celebrate achievements.
- Make it a habit to show gratitude and thank your staff often.
- Surprise a parent and phone to tell them how pleased you are about their child's results/behaviour.

Summary of Research Question 3
Staff, students and parents' results confirm that students are more motivated to learn when there is a positive school culture. Another benefit of a positive school culture acknowledged by all three groups was the improvement in relationships, especially between staff and students. All groups were in agreement that a positive culture promotes respectful interactions between staff and students. Another positive outcome raised by all three groups was that a positive culture improves student learning and that students want to come to school. It was evident from the results that all the groups believed that people are happier and students are treated well by teachers. Staff also indicated a positive school culture creates a sense of belonging and greater collaboration between staff. People feel valued and

there is less staff turnover. Less stress was raised by the staff as another benefit of a positive school culture, but was not mentioned by the students and parents. The students raised the following benefits that were not mentioned by the other groups: less bullying and that learning would be more enjoyable with a positive school culture.

Table 4.3 School Community's Response to Research Question 3

RQ 3 What are the perceived benefits of a positive school culture as identified by the school community?		
Principal and staff	**Students**	**Parents**
• both staff and students want to come to school; • creates a sense of belonging; • staff reported that they feel valued and appreciated; • collaboration between staff members is enhanced; • creates a more welcoming environment and builds better relationships; • less staff turnover; • students are treated well; • sense of belonging; • improves performance; • improves outcomes; • behaviour improves; and • less teacher stress.	• both students and staff would be happier; • less bullying; • improves relationships between teachers and students; • school would be a safer place; • people treat each other better; • makes learning fun; • encourages respectful relationships; • students perform better; • improve student learning; and • students are more motivated to learn.	• children perform better academically; • students enjoy school; • creates a more caring and safe environment; • promotes school improvement; • learning is more enjoyable; • creates a friendly, welcoming environment; • positive relationships with the students/staff; • more motivate to learn; • improves outcomes; • children are happier; and • fosters respectful interactions between staff and students.

3.5 Discussion of Research Question 4

What are the roles of the principal in establishing a positive school culture?

Introduction

The school community identified a variety of roles the principal has in cultivating a positive culture, including:

- leading by example;
- building relationships;
- leading the school;
- being an instructional leader;
- being a visionary leader; and
- being a leader of change and improvement.

Chapter 3: Discussion of Results

What are the roles of the principal in establishing a positive school culture?

The school community were able to identify that the principal has many roles in establishing a positive school culture. The list below shows the responses from the staff:

- have a positive outlook and be enthusiastic;
- support staff;
- model values and repeat the vision;
- needs to be seen as a leader and promote learning;
- attend school activities, visit the rooms and have a visible presence;
- remind school community of expectations;
- lead by example;
- encourage children and celebrate success;
- provide positive affirmations;
- ensure the students have a sense of belonging;
- listen to others to gain a solid understanding of issues;
- keep improving the school;
- help build relationships among members of the community;
- support school events and be approachable to discuss ideas and concerns;
- acknowledge and value each staff member's contribution;
- model how staff are to behave by words and actions; and
- encourage professional development to improve staff performance.

The principal believes that he plays a pivotal role in the cultivation of a positive school culture. He made the following points in regard to his leadership role:

- develops a vision of the school;
- guides the priorities and direction of the school;
- models behaviour, high expectations and values;
- ensures there are effective policies; procedures and personnel;
- promotes positive and respectful relationships;
- is a leader of learning;
- ensures the well-being of students and staff; and
- promotes professional learning cultures that work collaboratively to achieve goals.

In considering the roles undertaken by the principal, the parents believe that he plays a crucial role in the cultivation of a positive school culture and setting the direction for the vision for the school. The parents also raised the following points in regard to the role of the school principal:

- sets the expectations for the students;
- encourages staff and students to perform at their best;
- models the behaviour he wants;
- develops teamwork among staff;
- administers the school;
- promotes respectful relationships and builds relationships;
- celebrates achievement;
- empowers those around him;
- develops staff; and
- shapes and influences students.

Lead by example

The following response from the staff focus groups highlights the link between the vision of the school and the role of the school principal:

Both parents and staff believed that it was not enough to mention the mission statement, but that principals also needed to display virtues that are aligned with it. A finding from this research is that the principal plays a crucial role in the development of a positive school culture and that the principal would model how he wanted his staff to behave. This finding is also supported by Robinson (2015, p. 9) who writes, "Example will always be more important than words." This notion is also supported by Taylor (2015), who recommends that leaders must be an example of the behaviour they want others to display. The principal claims that every action he undertakes will either add to or detract from the culture of the school and therefore every interaction is an opportunity to influence the culture of the school.

In the interview with the principal, he stated that the virtues that are vital are trust, truth and honesty. The staff in the focus group and interviews believe a principal is required to have the following virtues: honesty; integrity; trustworthiness; enthusiasm; friendliness and positivity. Further, it was suggested by staff that for the school community to embrace the vision and values of the school, the principal is required to have a high level of emotional intelligence as indicated by a teacher in the following comment:

> *They need to be self-aware and reflective, genuine, friendly and positive themselves. Principals who are not social would find it very difficult to improve the culture of a school. The school principal has to be positive themselves. They need to have an optimistic approach and be self-aware. They need to have a high degree of emotional intelligence. (Teacher 1)*

A finding from this research is that the principal plays a crucial role in the development of a positive school culture. This is in agreement with the observations made by James and Connelly (2008) that the principal plays an important role in shaping the culture of the school and the overall performance of the school they lead.

Relationship builder

The staff responses indicate that the principal role requires a high level of people skills and trust. In this respect, Watkins (2005, p. 83) emphasises why principals need to make the promotion of relationships a priority with the statement, "Relationships are not just important, but are the very foundation of the organisation, the fabric of the team. No individual can do it alone." In this research staff suggested that an important role for the principal was to engage with parents and build relationships so that teachers and students could develop positive relationships. They required the principal to be both supportive and treat people fairly. The principal notes that an important part of his role was to promote positive and respectful relationships between staff and students. The students acknowledged that the principal built relationships with them by talking to them, visiting classrooms and attending school events. They also suggested that an important aspect of the principal's role was being responsible for the care and well-being of students and staff. This result confirms the importance of principals in building relationships and responding effectively when listening to others, especially when staff go to seek help or advice.

School leader

The students identified a variety of roles the principal has in cultivating a positive school culture: reminding students of the values and expectations; being involved in classroom activities; leading assemblies; focusing on teacher performance; caring for students and being responsible for discipline. Other roles the principal acknowledges include: to ensure the well-being of the students; insist on high standards; be a leader of learning; develop a collaborative culture; promote positive staff and student relationships; and maintain a positive culture. The principal compares himself to that of a painter in that they colour all aspects of the school through their actions and words. In this research, as indicated in the results, the principal must be enthusiastic and display a positive attitude. The principal indicated that the leadership role was a privilege and he thoroughly enjoyed taking an active role in the learning. The principal believes school leaders are required to have the skills in setting up the procedures, policies and leadership structures so that the school is administered effectively.

Instructional leader

The principal acknowledges that as the head teacher, he has a crucial role to influence others around him. The school community indicated that improving the quality of teaching performance was seen as part of the principal's role, this included supporting the professional development of staff. Hargreaves and Fullan (2012) recommend that principals need to stay connected with teachers and must also embrace learning themselves. A high priority for the principal was the development of a learning culture. The importance of professional development is supported by Khalil, Kalim and Abiodullah (2013) who report that professional development plays a decisive role in uplifting the quality and performance of any institution or organisation. The results from the principal's interview indicate that the first priority of the school principal should be the students' learning. The principal's response concurs with that of Jensen et al. (2015), who argue that the school leaders' greatest impact is achieved through leading effective teacher learning. In this respect one of the most important aspects of the principal's role is concerned with student learning and teacher performance. The principal's focus on learning and teacher development is supported by Khalil, Kalim and Abiodullah's (2013) research that successful and effective schools have high-level professional learning communities.

Visionary leader

The ACGCEO (2009) leadership framework asserts that principals need to regularly articulate vision and goals to the school community. The principal in this research recognised that the school leader's input was vital to the direction of the school. The principal himself indicated the need for school leaders to give staff direction and a clear focus. The principal shared how he communicated the vision with the school community as indicated in this response:

> *I often bring in articles for staff to think about and challenge them. I try and present information in different formats and not in the same way, stating the intent or vision of the school. You need to present the message in a variety of ways.* (Principal)

This accords with the findings of Hargreaves and Fullan (2012) who note that positive cultures can assist in the development of professional teachers working collectively under visionary leadership so that all students can succeed. It is evident from the results that parents believe that the principal needs to model how he wants people to act and behave. The staff felt that an important role for the school principal was repeating the school vision and ethos. These findings are similar to those of Fullan (2010) that when people work together, this generates commitment for the collective good. Watkins (2005) asserts that a school's vision defines what the school seeks to be, not what it is. He recommends that members of the school should participate in the creation of the vision so that it will inspire and motivate members of the school community to work toward achieving it. Stronge et al. (2013) acknowledge that an effective leader involves the whole school when creating a safe and positive learning environment. The findings from this research support the observations made by Rhodes et al. (2011) who pronounce that principals play pivotal roles in the production and maintenance of school cultures. The parents also suggested that the principal not only sets the tone of the school but the priorities for staff and students. The Ontario Ministry of Education (2010) also supports this view and states that school leaders set the tone for their schools. They also reported that the principal sets the goals and priorities for the school.

Leader of change and improvement

It is evident from the research results that student performance is influenced by the school principal. The staff and parents mentioned the importance of the principal's role in developing teamwork and teacher performance to improve student learning. As pointed out by Jensen and Reichl (2011), increased teacher effectiveness can improve student performance by as much as 20 to 30%. They argue that better teachers are the key to producing higher-performing students. The staff asserted that the principal's role was to keep improving the school and the skills of the staff. This result is in line with previously considered findings from the principal. Gurr's (2015) research confirmed the core leadership practices, including: setting direction, developing people; leading change and improving teaching and learning. Taylor (2015) contends that changing a culture is a team process. The parents believe the principal sets the standards and the school's expectations, and the students recommended that he must continue to focus on the way teachers teach so that they are doing a good job. The parents felt an important role for the principal was to encourage staff and students to perform at their best and this is supported by Masters (2010) stating that effective leaders create cultures of high expectations that lead to ongoing efforts to improve teaching practices. As can be seen from the findings of this research, each group indicated the importance of the principal focusing upon teacher performance. The students also observed that the principal should remind everyone of the school's expectations.

> *The principal needs to keep looking at how we can improve. Just because something worked once does not mean it will continue to work. Next time it may not work at all. It means never being totally satisfied or happy with what is happening so you are continually searching for ways to improve the school.*
> (Head of Department 1)

Reflective questions

- From the staff list, what do you think are the most important roles/tasks of the principal?
- In what ways does the school encourage children and celebrate success?
- In what ways do you support professional development at school?
- What are the key actions/values you need to model to your school community?

Decisive actions

- Refer back to the principal's points in regard to his leadership role. List in order your priorities from his recommendations.
- Explore how you can communicate your expectations and goals more effectively.
- Discuss with the leadership team how they can inspire others to respond positively and to motivate the school community to work together as a team.
- With staff, create a list of core values, behaviours and actions important to them that constitute a positive workplace.

Summary of Research Question 4

The next table shows that the school community identified many roles of the school principal that would assist in the cultivation of a positive school culture. There were several recommended behaviours from the leadership framework (ACGCEO, 2009) that matched the responses in Table 3.4, including: pursue constant and continuous improvement; place high priority on the development of mature relationships; promote life-long learning; regularly focus the community on a clearly articulated vision and set of goals; model participation in professional learning; and work toward creating shared expectations and understandings. It was noted from all the groups responses that the principal is a role model and is required to lead by example. The parents added that the principal's actions and words must support the school's vision and values. The staff also believed that the principal is required to focus upon the vision and goals of the school. Another important role recognised by all the groups was that the principal be responsible for the performance of the teachers and improving teaching standards. The results from all three groups for this question indicated that a very important role of the school principal is relationship builder.

Table 3.4 School Community's Response to Research Question 4

RQ 4 What are the roles of the principal in establishing a positive school culture?		
Principal and staff	**Students**	**Parents**
• focus upon school improvement; • improving the area of teaching and student learning; • a relationship builder; • focus upon the vision and goals; • reinforce the standards and expectations; • effective communicator; • acknowledge the effort of staff and students and express gratitude often; • role model; and • uniting people toward achieving a common purpose.	• fix things that were causing problems; • visit the classrooms; • role model; • being responsible for everyone's well-being and safety; • ensuring people are happy; • ensuring students and staff are following rules; • improve teacher performance; • build relationships; • smiling and being friendly; and • getting to know the students.	• ensuring that the children perform academically; • setting the tone of the school; • developing a team approach; • improving student learning; • building relationships; • leading by example; • actions and words must support vision; • providing a safe environment; • actions must reflect values; • improving teacher standards; • focusing upon the vision of the school; and • being supportive of the students.

A further result demonstrated from staff and parent responses was that the principal needs to focus their attention on improving student learning and overall school improvement. It can be seen from the table that there was agreement between the three groups about the principal setting the expectations and ensuring standards are being met. Staff and parents agreed that a role of the principal was uniting people to have a team approach to achieve the school's vision and goals. All the groups acknowledge the visible presence the principal displayed and made comments about him attending so many school events. The students suggested the principal ensures everyone's safety and is responsible for their well-being. It can be seen from Table 3.4 that the principalship is complex, due to the diverse roles expected of the principal.

3.6 Discussion of Research Question 5

What are the recommendations from the school community for the cultivation of a positive school culture?

Introduction

The school community was able to suggest many strategies that the principal could implement to cultivate a positive school culture. It was evidenced from the results that the principal was using most of the following recommendations:

- examine the school's existing culture;
- role-model the values;
- make the cultivation of a positive school culture a high priority;
- be visible;
- be approachable and available;
- be positive and enthusiastic;
- develop relationships;
- ensure the school vision is supported by all school community members;
- utilise a distributed leadership approach;
- promote a professional learning culture;
- appoint quality staff;
- focus on school improvement; and
- implement procedures and policies that cultivate a positive culture.

Examine the school's existing culture

Chapter 2 suggests principals use knowledge from a variety of sources to make informed decisions. The principal's interview highlights the importance placed on collecting data and advocated the use of this data to gain a clear understanding of what was working well within the school. This supports research that suggests that a principal's success will be influenced by their understanding of their school's culture (Keiser & Schulte 2009; Ontario Ministry of Education, 2010). The findings from this research support the observations made by Hargreaves and Shirley (2009) that schools can become better learning organisations when teachers use data to inform their decisions, monitor student progress and adjust their teaching accordingly. These authors recommend that staff use multiple data sources to assist staff with their decision making.

Lead by example and role-model the values

The ACGCEO (2009) leadership framework asserts that truly effective school leaders demonstrate ethically responsible behaviour. This assertion aligns with the following staff recommendation that the principal be a role model and set a good example for the school community, and also confirms Taylor's (2015) reflection that values are what drive the behaviour in the workplace. Leaders must therefore model the school's values and articulate them often so that these are embedded in the school culture (Edwards & Martin, 2016). The founder of the Sisters of Mercy, Catherine McAuley, placed great importance on how teachers should behave and thus, the example they set (Mercy College, 2014). The parents believed that the principal is required to model the ethos and communicate the school's vision and expectations. This supports findings by Zbar, Kimber and Marshall (2008) who found that leaders of top-performing schools set high expectations for teaching and learning and would then model these expectations to the staff. The principal spoke about how every interaction influences how people in the school behave. This is supported by Sharp (2014) who recommends that those who want to improve the culture at their workplace need to lead by example.

> *Without trying to sound too clichéd, the fish stinks from the head down. It starts from the top. The principal has a major effect by the modelling aspect, every interaction you have is leading the culture, and every interaction I have like talking to someone, all impacts upon the culture. It is almost if you have a barometer on you which tells others your values, what you believe in.* (Principal)

Make the cultivation of a positive school culture a high priority

The principal recommended that the cultivation of a positive school culture be a priority for the school community. This result is consistent with Taylor's (2015) conclusion that culture has to be owned and driven by leaders and their people. Moore (2009) advocates for school leaders to focus on school culture because it has a direct impact on student achievement. Hargreaves and Fullan (2012) recommend that principals model the changes they want to see in their schools. Taylor (2015) notes that for organisations to be successful during significant change, culture needs to be a high priority.

Be visible, approachable and available

As shown in the results, the staff wanted a principal who was visible, approachable and accessible. The principal walked around the school each day and this allowed him to have a firm grasp of what was happening. These conclusions are similar to those of Marzano, Waters and McNulty (2005) who found that principals who were able to establish positive cultures within their schools typically visited classrooms and established close ties with the stakeholders of the school. Being visible in the school is a core leadership practice (Gurr, 2014) and some staff indicated that principals who are involved in doing the work of the people they lead had more credibility. The responses from these staff members concur with Pfeffer and Sutton (2000, p. 58) who state, "People cannot complain about a boss who does not understand their problems and issues when the boss does many of the same activities."

They need to be serving on the counter; they need to out there in the classroom and the playground. They need to be seen and not stuck in their office. They need to be visible in and around the school. I think having a presence is a big thing. (Parent 1)

Principal needs to be positive and enthusiastic

The ACGCEO (2009) leadership framework highlights the behaviours of highly effective principals which are similar to the findings from this research. For example, a supporting behaviour from Table 1.2 states that principals need to affirm, praise and give constructive feedback to others. Even though the framework does not emphasise the cultivation of a positive school culture, the listed behaviours of effective principals are aligned with the findings of this research. The results confirmed that the principal excelled at being positive and enthusiastic. It is evident from the responses that the

He praises people all the time. He doesn't focus on the negative but looks for what went right and searches for the positive. He looks for what is right in a situation or person. If someone makes a mistake he says, "What can we learn from this? And how can we do it better next time?" (Administration 2)

principal emphasises the importance of principals using positive language when dealing with staff, especially when addressing an issue. The principal believes leaders need to be unfailingly positive, lavish in their praise and slow in showing aggravation. This result supports the strategy of principals using positive language to create a positive culture. This result also confirmed research undertaken by Taylor, Jenkins & Barber (2013) that leaders should be careful when giving people feedback as they believe that criticism can easily become destructive. This idea is supported by Seligman (2011) who warns against the negative feedback most people are given in appraisals as it does not promote change. Instead, he recommends people be told what is best about them and how they can use their strengths more, as they are more likely to change with a more positive approach.

Build positive relationships and promote a friendly environment

The ACGCEO (2009) leadership framework identifies that effective principals place a high priority on the development of relationships. The results in this research support the literature in The Education Review Office (2008) who report that successful schools invested time and energy in providing a range of interactive opportunities to build collegiality among staff and good relationships with parents and students. This result is also similar to that of Hargreaves and Shirley (2009) who believe teacher happiness comes from developing and achieving goals in positive relationships with colleagues. The staff suggested that the principal build the relationships he needs to develop by: showing an interest in the staff; being involved with school activities; making time for others; being approachable and being positive. To promote a positive school culture, the parents recommended that the principal provide support to members of the school community and promote positive, respectful relationships between students and staff. Fullan (2002) observed that as relationships improve within the school community, the school culture becomes more positive.

> *Building relationships and setting the tone for the school and valuing people is very important.* (School Board Member 2)

Implement procedures and policies that cultivate a positive culture

This research shows that the principal utilised many strategies to create a successful school. The results of this research are supported by Caldwell and Harris (2008) who argue that success is achieved through the alignment of many strategies and the research shows that the principal utilised many strategies to create a successful school culture. Sharp (2014) observes that most people acknowledge that it would be beneficial to make the cultivation of a positive culture in their workplace a priority, but few people are actually committed to developing it. Hargreaves and Fullan (2012) believe that teaching is profoundly affected by the environment and the existing culture of the workplace and, similarly, Caldwell and Harris (2008) report that schools can make a significant improvement in student performance by having a culture of high expectations.

Utilise a distributed leadership approach

This recommendation from the school community supports the ACGCEO (2009) leadership framework, which states that principals need to nurture leadership capability in others. In this research, the principal was a strong advocate for utilising a distributed leadership approach which is supported by Fullan's (2005) findings and warns against principals being the only decision maker in the school. According to Fullan (2010), and Duignan and Cannon (2011), learning is a joint effort of many people working together for a moral purpose. The same authors recommend principals distribute their leadership tasks, due to the complexity and multidimensionality of the principal's role. Gurr's (2015) results found that successful school leaders who practised a distributed leadership model would often acknowledge that the success of their school was due to the leadership of many others within the school.

Schools to have a moral purpose

The results indicate that the principal's focus was on the well-being of the students. The principal also spoke about the need for the staff to have a shared moral purpose and to collectively support the vision and values of the school. Fullan (2010), and Hargreaves and Shirley (2009), talk about school communities all having a moral purpose of high expectations for all students and believing that all students can learn.

Chapter 3: Discussion of Results

Develop a team approach by staff to implement school's vision and goals

The staff suggested that the principal maintain the vision of the school. The principal believes that the success and culture of the school depends on how individuals in the school are able to work together to achieve the school's goals. The results indicate that a strength of the principal was his ability to communicate effectively to the school community. The results in this research support observations by Taylor (2015) that cooperative cultures develop in a community who have shared goals, beliefs, routines and values,

> *Staff can't work in a vacuum; they need direction on what to focus on. The individual's actions therefore are more aligned and consistent with the school's vision, which filters down to the kids.*
> (Principal)

and who recommends that leaders need to communicate the goals, values and rules so that everyone has a clear understanding of what is expected of them. The results reveal that an important priority of the school principal is to encourage all members of the school community to have a team approach toward achieving the school's goals. As highlighted in the principal's interview, he stated that staff cannot work in a vacuum and need direction on what to focus on and be aligned to what the school's vision and goals are. This result confirms observations by Fullan (2010) who suggests schools will not get the results they want unless the teachers are committed to the vision and expectations of the school. This observation also supports the principal's recommendation that school leaders need to establish clear guidelines so that staff know what behaviours are expected of them to be able to work effectively and align their actions with the school's vision.

Develop a professional learning culture

This recommendation from the school community is aligned with the ACGCEO (2009) leadership framework which states that a core capability for school principals is to be committed to continuous learning. It recommends that principals develop a culture of continuous learning and encourage the acquisition of new skills. During his interview, the principal demonstrated strong support for staff development, and the importance of principals leading the learning and promoting a culture of learning. The above results are consistent with the findings of Khalil, Kalim and Abiodullah (2013), who suggest that a school culture that values professional development, meaningful co-curricular activities and student achievement, provides a thriving platform for students and staff excellence. Hargreaves and Fullan (2012) recommend that teachers continuously seek to improve their skills so that the performance of the entire team increases. The Productivity Commission (2012) highlights the critical role of quality teaching and the importance of deploying quality teachers effectively across schools. Fullan (2010) states that every top-performing system has focused upon improving the entire teaching profession. Watkins (2005) suggests that good leaders keep student learning as a focus of their work. School leadership has shifted from doing only the management of the school to improving student outcomes with Duignan and Cannon (2011) recommending that school leadership teams focus on leading the teaching and building professional learning communities.

Develop a collaborative culture

The principal proposes that staff need a healthy understanding of what a collaborative culture is, including what is expected of them. This is supported by Hargreaves and Fullan (2012), who found that collaborative cultures are places of hard work and dedication which lead to a sense of collective responsibility and pride in the school. They add that collaborative schools do better than individualistic ones. The principal's recommendations for the cultivation of a positive school culture include developing a team approach to reaching the school's goals and vision. The results suggest that there is agreement with the following supporting behaviour listed in Chapter 2, *builds a sharing organisational culture that harnesses energies and talents*. According to Taylor (2015), teams are the backbone of an organisation's culture and need to have clear goals, purposes and roles. Barnett and McCormick (2012) recommend that leaders move away from leader-centred organisations to team-centred ones. They add that leaders must develop leadership capabilities of staff so that they can effectively share these responsibilities.

Hire quality staff

The principal acknowledged that the quality of staff had a significant impact on the school's performance and placed much emphasis on recruiting the most suitable applicant for the school. However, the school's location made this difficult. As stated earlier, a significant challenge for the principal was hiring quality staff who will support the ethos of the school. Caldwell and Harris' (2008) research findings highlight the importance of schools recruiting and selecting quality teachers and non-teaching staff. Pfeffer and Sutton (2000) recommend that companies must treat

> *If kids are happy and staff are happy within a school and respect each other the learning is much improved. If you have a positive culture then learning is so much better. Positivity makes things work better.*
> (Head of Department 2)

their people as if they really matter, which they believe means taking care of their employees. Taylor (2015) warns that organisations that continue to have poor cultures will have difficulty in attracting the best people and will fall further behind due to people's preference to move to better workplaces.

Focus on school improvement

The ACGCEO leadership framework states that effective school leaders pursue constant and continuous improvement (2009, p. 3) which supports the findings from the results. The staff recommended that the principal continue to focus on school improvement. Hargreaves and Fullan (2012)

> *I feel proud to be part of a team and I love working in a great place.*
> (Administration 1)

observe that good learning comes from good teaching and recommend that great effort is needed in this area to attract and produce the best teachers. They add that education systems must maximise the cumulative effect of improving all teachers over time and that this will transform the entire teaching profession. The students recommended the principal keep improving the teaching standards and that the principal ensures that they are happy with what they are learning. Habegger (2008, p. 42) writes, "Positive school culture is the heart of improvement and growth."

Reflective questions
- How does the school collect data to gain a clear understanding of what is working well within the school?
- What aspect of your leadership gives you the most satisfaction?
- How could you be more visible or accessible to your school community?
- How do you encourage all members of the school community to have a team approach toward achieving the school's goals?
- How do staff know you value them?

Decisive actions
- Ask your school community what strategies they could implement to cultivate a positive school culture.
- Using the Positive School Culture Improvement Tool, discuss with your staff/leadership team what recommendations could be implemented in your own situation. Remember to only implement a few recommendations effectively before utilising more recommendations.
- Explore ways you can be more positive and enthusiastic. Regularly meet with a mentor/colleague to share ideas over a coffee.

Summary of Research Question 5

The effective behaviours from the leadership framework (ACGCEO, 2009) that matched the responses in Table 3.5 include the following: successful leaders are learners; frequently stands up for beliefs; shows a positive and confident approach to leadership; at all times, leaders are concerned about right relationships; possesses high-level understanding of group dynamics and generates maximum performance from all staff members; facilitates positive and collaborative relationships; is approachable, trustworthy and acts pastorally toward others; and endorses a climate of sharing and support utilising the expertise of individuals. In relation to RQ 5, the results have demonstrated that the school community wants a principal who has a visible presence around the school and who attends school events. The principal also needs to have a positive attitude and be approachable. These recommendations were behaviours that the principal was highly competent in displaying and allowed him to build relationships with members of the school community. The results also demonstrate the importance of the principal communicating the vision and expectations of the school.

Table 3.5 School Community's Response to Research Question 5

RQ 5 What are the recommendations from the school community for the cultivation of a positive school culture?		
Principal and staff	**Students**	**Parents**
• Focus on school improvement; • unfailingly positive; • role-model the values; • be a leader of learning; • develop relationships; • positive culture a priority; • use positive language; • implement a distributed leadership model; • being active; • having a visible presence; • ensure a collaborative culture; • attend school activities; and • be approachable.	• spending time talking with the students; • being positive and happy; • showing enthusiasm; • visit the classrooms; • be supportive; • be friendly; • visible around the school; • attend events and activities; and • take time listening to students.	• be approachable; • engage parents in conversation; • be visible around the school; • establish clear rules; • team approach to decisions; • attend school events; and • be friendly.

A further result demonstrated that the school community expects the school principal to role-model the values of the school. The students and parents suggested that the principal is required to be friendly. The students also stated that the principal listens to students and visits classrooms. Chapter 4 makes conclusions from the results and presents recommendations for school principals who would like to cultivate a positive school culture within their own schools. This chapter also presents implications of the research and identifies areas for further research.

3.7 Discussion of Research Question 6

What are the characteristics or behaviours of an excellent school principal?

Introduction

The question for this theme explored the school community's perceptions about the principal's enthusiasm, behaviour and virtues. The school community were asked to identify the characteristics or behaviours that define an excellent principal.

Table 3.6 – The school community's responses to the following question – *What are the characteristics or behaviours of an excellent school principal?*

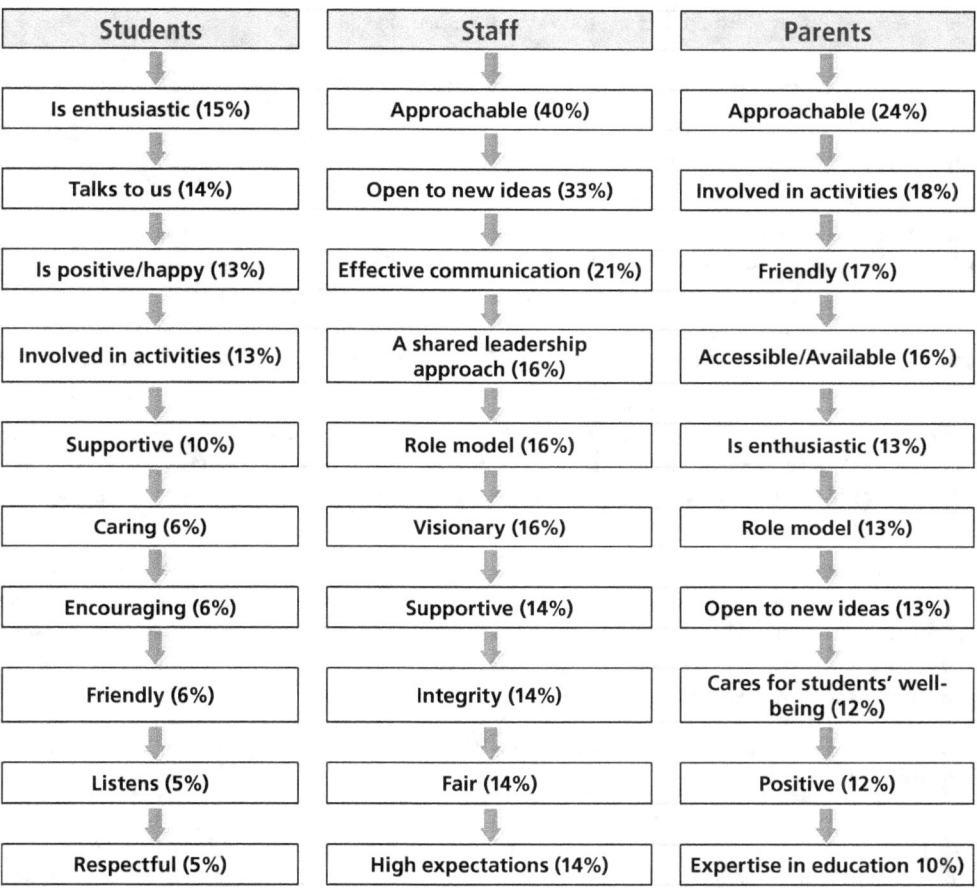

Table 3.6 presents the most common responses from the school community in regard to what they thought were the characteristics or behaviours of an excellent school principal. These included: approachable; effective communication; open to new ideas; enthusiastic; involved in activities; role model; enthusiastic; positive/happy; supportive; friendly and caring. This table shows that *approachable* was the highest response from both the staff (40%) and parent (24%) respondents. *Open to new ideas* (33%) and *effective communication* (21%) also rated highly with the staff. Being a role model was also viewed as important with the staff and parents. According to staff, the principal has a significant role in shaping the school culture. They believe he sets the tone and his actions will demonstrate how he

expects his staff to behave. Staff expect many things of the principal, not least being a role model and a support. Another important aspect of the principalship the staff identified was the need for the principal to respect and value each staff member's contribution by taking the time to talk to staff. These perceptions are illustrated in the following statements:

> *I think it is to be a role model. Everything the principal asks of his staff and the students he demonstrates himself.* (Head of Department 3)

> *He daily sets the tone and his expectations for the school and how he expects us to behave.* (Teacher 1)

Like the staff, the parents commented upon the importance of the school principal being a role model. The parents also acknowledge how the principal's words and actions influenced the people around him. They observed that the principal was able to see the good qualities in others and supported them in achieving their goals. The parents emphasised the importance of the principal being accessible and indicated that it was at times frustrating if this was restricted. These perceptions are highlighted in the following response:

> *Parents need to be able to meet with the principal. On occasions, we have asked to see the principal and we can't get past the front desk. They ask us to meet with someone else. We can't get past the front office to talk to and see the principal. He needs to be available to parents.* (Parent volunteer 2)

The parents responded to the eighty different suggestions as to what the characteristics or behaviours of an excellent school principal were. The parents recognise the principal's involvement by his *attending* school activities, with 40% of parent respondents mentioning this. The principal being both accessible (20%) and *approachable* (19%) was also seen as important. The following statement is typical of the responses made by the parent group:

> *At every school event, he is front and centre. He is always friendly, inclusive and passionately involved.* (Parent)

In Table 3.6 the students' question was simplified to: *What makes our school principal excellent?* Table 3.6 shows that fifteen per cent (15%) of the students and thirteen per cent (13%) of parents referred to *enthusiasm* in their responses. The students gave 53 different responses, with *talks to us* (14%); is *positive/happy* (13%) and *involved in activities* (13%) as among the most common responses. The following responses to the question demonstrate how the students describe an excellent principal:

> *Our school principal is always enthusiastic and encouraging.* (Student)

> *He goes around through the classes and talks to the students and cares about what they have to say.* (Student)

Chapter 3: Discussion of Results

Staff observed that the more positive and upbeat the principal was, the more staff and students want to come to school. The principal's mood was almost contagious. When the school community experienced positive emotions from the principal this made them feel positive. This is aligned with Fredrickson's (2009) research suggesting that the mood of the leadership impacted on the people they were leading. It was also found that the group of people they managed was influenced by their positivity and this group produced better efficiency and displayed greater coordination. Parents mentioned that they want their children and staff to be happy. The students also mentioned that the principal always seems happy and walked around with a smile on his face, as seen in the following example statements:

He always has a smile on his face and he always seems happy. (Year 10 student)

He seems like a guy that you can relate to, like he always seems happy. (Year 10 student)

When discussing leadership, the student focus group often acknowledged the principal's presence at many school events. This was valued by the students and was felt to be important, as seen in the following response:

He makes an effort to turn up to a lot of things like the assemblies. He will be there every Wednesday and plays a major part of it as well. He always has a speech even if it goes a bit long sometimes. You know he always makes an effort. He always comes down to the sporting games and goes on camps. (Year 10 student)

Students also mentioned that he reminds them at assemblies of the importance of treating others with respect. Assemblies were often the time when he would highlight students' efforts and would praise them publicly. The principal would also remind the students of the school's expectation and the students appreciated his visits to their classrooms. Evidence of these experiences is illustrated in the following quotes:

He comes around to the classrooms and talks to you. And not every principal does that. (Year 10 student)

Even in my French class he will join in the activity and try to speak French, even though he can't speak it well. (Year 10 student)

How has the principal built positive relationships?

Table 3.7 present the five highest responses (in descending order) to the question and the percentage of that response that came from the staff, students and parents. The respondents were encouraged to give three responses to the following question: How has the principal built positive relationships?

Table 3.7 – The school community's responses to the following question – *How has the principal built positive relationships?*

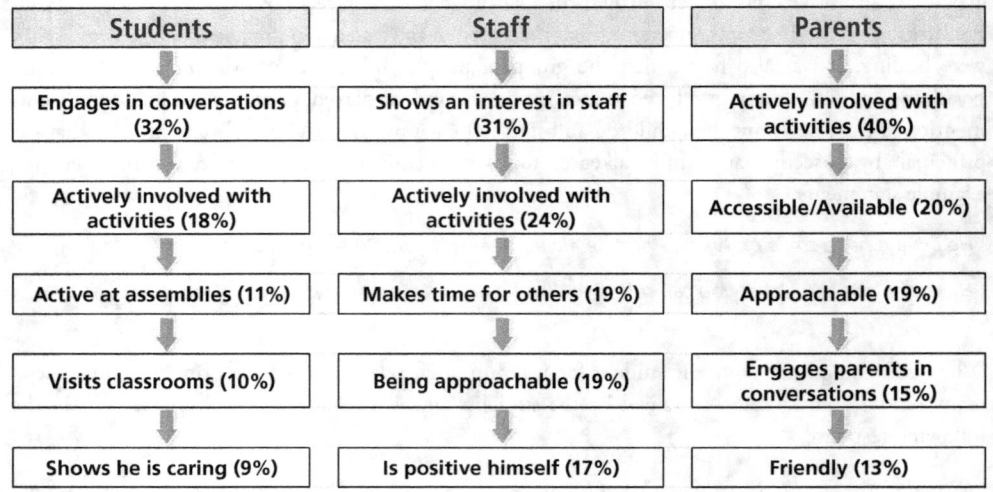

The staff gave sixty 60 different suggestions to how the principal has built positive relationships. The most common response was the principal *showing an interest in the staff* (31%) and *being involved with school activities* (24%). The following statements from the staff were typical of responses.

> He is positive himself. Leading through service and by example. He knows his staff and has an understanding of each person. This makes each staff member feel valued. (Staff)
>
> By being approachable, friendly and open with staff. Showing a genuine interest in all areas. (Staff)

As shown in Table 3.7, thirty-two per cent (32%) of students mentioned how the principal engages the students in conversations. The students gave fifty different responses. The other most common responses were: actively engages with activities (18%); active at assemblies (11%); visits classrooms (10%); and shows he is caring (9%).

The parents recognise the principal attending school events with forty per cent (40%) mentioning the principal's involvement at school activities. Parents also rate highly the principal being available (20%), closely followed by being approachable (19%). The parents' results suggest that principals engage with parents (15%) and need to be friendly (13%).

The following statements are typical of the responses made by the students about how the principal has built positive relationships:

Chapter 3: Discussion of Results

The principal is at pretty much every school event and makes an effort to always engage in conversation with us. He is respectful, friendly, and treats us like adults rather than children which is much appreciated. (Student)

Interesting talks at assembly – visits classes regularly – participates in activities – makes an effort to know everyone in the school – is encouraging and wants everyone to do well. (Student)

Summary

The principal was seen as very supportive, especially his presence at many extra-curricular activities. The students observed that the principal is almost always happy as he walks around the school and visits classrooms. Many students mentioned his attendance at assemblies and award nights. At public occasions, he would be either reminding students of his expectations or the majority of times celebrating some student achievement. A noteworthy observation was that he always has a smile on his face. The students also commented upon the principal knowing each student's name and encouraging them to be the best they can be. The parents' perception of the current principal was very positive and of the example he sets for the staff and students. A concern raised by parents was the principal not being accessible due to procedures at the front office restricting access. The parents felt he must not only be accessible but also approachable. The principal's attendance at the many school events was recognised and appreciated.

The principal has many roles, not least being a role model to the rest of staff. His behaviour shapes the behaviour of the school community and ultimately the culture of the school. The staff acknowledged his positive attitude and enthusiasm. To create a positive culture the principal must be positive. The principal maintains that he be a leader of learning and also build relationships with members of the school community. Due to the complexity of the role, the staff, parents and principal advocate for a distributed leadership approach. The principal was an effective leader as he was able to maximise the performance of the staff by improving their individual capacity and their ability to work together to achieve the school's goals.

Reflective questions

- What do you think are the behaviours and characteristics of an excellent school principal?
- What are three virtues that guide your leadership?
- What are three actions that you do that your school community values?
- Is there any virtue or action you need to focus on?
- What behaviour do you need to role-model to staff to improve the school?
- How does the leadership team support staff?
- How do you build relationships with students?

Decisive actions

- Review Table 3.6. List your signature strengths.
- Discuss with staff how the leadership team can support them better in achieving their goals.
- Explore ways you can be more accessible to your school community.
- Which strategy in Table 3.7 would assist you most in building relationships with members of your school community? Now implement it!
- Discuss with a colleague how they unite their school community to work more effectively.
- Explore the messages your leadership team are communicating about having high expectations to the staff, students and parents. Ensure the school community has a good understanding about what is valued in your school.

Chapter 4
Conclusions and Recommendations

4.1 Introduction

This book has presented a case study that explores the role of the principal in the cultivation of a positive school culture in a secondary-school setting. An extensive search of literature revealed that there is limited research concerning leadership and positive school culture in an Australian context. This chapter presents conclusions from the research into the role of the school principal in the cultivation of a positive school culture. Then, arising out of the research, a set of recommendations for principals and school communities is presented. Lastly, this chapter provides concluding remarks.

4.2 Conclusions

Introduction

The results from the data collection instruments have provided a rich description of the principal's role regarding cultivating a positive school culture. The following six conclusions can be made from this research.

- Results from this research indicate the specific aspects of school and school community that contribute to a positive school culture. Namely: treating each other respectfully; having a friendly school community; the presence of positive relationships between members of the school community; school's values and vision being known to all; everyone having high expectations of each other; students displaying good behaviour; the principal having a positive and enthusiastic attitude; the need for an engaging curriculum; students having a sense of belonging; aesthetics of the school being of a high standard; the principal modelling the behaviour he wants others to display; the school environment being safe and caring; and having high job satisfaction by staff.
- This research has demonstrated that there are many challenges faced by the school principal in cultivating a positive school culture. Specifically, the main challenges are: maintaining a positive school culture; the school community working collaboratively toward the school's vision and goals; attracting and retaining high-quality staff; developing teachers as leaders; promoting change; assisting staff in a demanding teaching environment; developing positive relationships between all members of the school community; and improving student learning.

This research has demonstrated that there are many benefits of a positive school culture. Many of these confirm previous research that is reported in the literature. These include: students and staff are more motivated to learn; obtaining high student academic achievement; increase the level of collaboration between members of the school community; promotes positive relationships; both staff and students want to be at the school; creating a more positive workplace; improving student behaviour; and leaders having a positive focus.

- The literature presented in Chapter 2 indicated that the principal has many roles. Many of these roles have been similarly found and have been elaborated upon in this research. Namely, establishing a positive school culture include: lead by example; relationship builder; school leader; instructional leader; visionary leader and leader of change and improvement.
- There are many actions that a school principal can implement that will assist in the cultivation of a positive school culture as suggested by the school community. The recommendations from the school community for the cultivation of a positive school culture included the following: examine the school's existing culture; role-model the values; make the cultivation of a positive school culture a high priority; be visible; be approachable and available; be positive and enthusiastic; develop relationships; ensure the school vision is supported by all school community members; utilise a distributed leadership approach; promote a professional learning culture; appoint quality staff; focus on school improvement; and implement procedures and policies that cultivate a positive culture.

The ACGCEO (2009) leadership framework presented in Chapter 1 identified fifteen capabilities and associated supporting behaviours that assist principals in their role. This research has demonstrated that the recommended supporting behaviours, as identified in the framework, were implemented by the principal to assist him in his role in cultivating a positive school culture. These include: affirms, praises and gives constructive feedback; actively promotes values and traditions; nurtures leadership capability in others; engages in learning and professional development; models and encourages a strong achievement orientation in others; and builds collegial purpose and vision for the school. The behaviours from the framework that were not identified in this research included faith and spiritual development. The following section further considers the conclusions from this research.

4.3 The Key Behaviours of the Principal that Assist with the Cultivation of a Positive School Culture

This research has identified the behaviours by the principal that assist and help maintain a positive school culture, as discussed in Chapter 2.

Chapter 4: Conclusions and Recommendations

Figure 4.1 Key Behaviours of the Principal to Cultivate a Positive School Culture

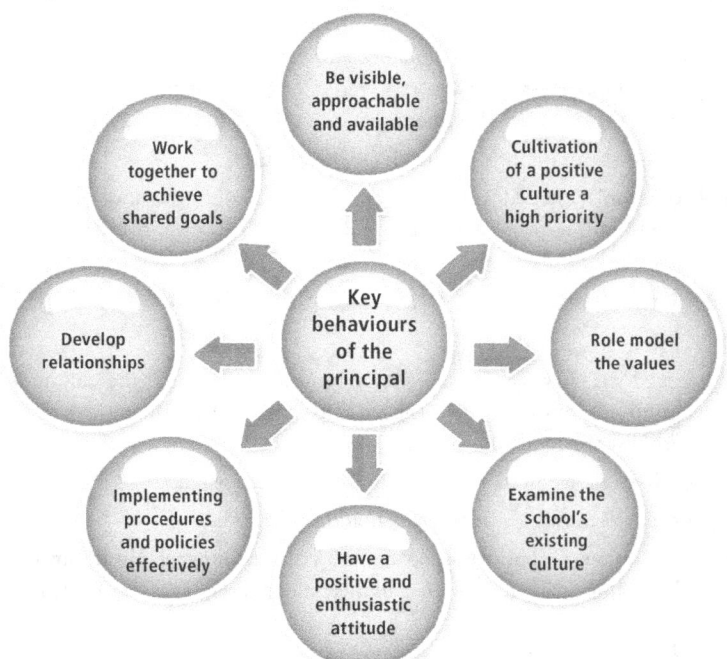

While the behaviours are consistent with those reported in the literature this research has detailed, more specifically, a number of behaviours that can be interpreted as critical to the cultivation of a positive school culture. This specifically concerns the importance of the principal uniting the school community to work together to achieve shared goals. The remainder of this section elaborates on these key behaviours.

Examining the school's existing culture

In this research, the principal examined the existing school culture by:

- conducting a school review;
- walking through the playground and visiting the classrooms; and
- encouraging staff to be guided by data and then implementing changes in relation to the examination of the data.

The principal constantly examined what was actually working (and not working) within the school. This behaviour by the principal is similar to the recommendation in the leadership framework which states principals are required to read and analyse situations accurately.

Role-modelling the values
The ACGCEO (2009) framework highlighted the importance of principals consistently displaying and articulating their understanding of the values and vision of the school. In this research, it was found that the principal modelled what was expected of others, allowing him to lead the culture and influencing it to create the school environment that he wanted. The principal considered that:
- every interaction was an opportunity to shape the culture;
- the school community needed to be reminded of the school's goals and values; and the staff treat the students with respect – and the principal modelled this himself.

Make the cultivation of a positive school culture a high priority
The principal believed that having a positive school culture maximised the children's learning. He demonstrated a sound educational focus. The principal made the cultivation of a positive school culture a high priority by the following actions:
- having clear expectations on how staff are to interact with students;
- fostering positive relationships between staff and students; and
- making the cultivation of a positive school culture a continuous goal. He acknowledged that every action he did was influencing the culture and therefore modelled want he wanted others to do.

Being visible, approachable and available to all members of the school community
The supporting behaviours mentioned in Chapter 2 advocate for principals to actively listen and show an interest in the views of others within the school community. The findings of this research showed the importance of the principal being approachable, as noted by both parents and staff. The principal had a visible presence by:
- visiting the classrooms each day; and
- attending all school activities.

By having a positive and enthusiastic attitude
As noted in the ACGCEO (2009) leadership framework, principals should be required to act with positive regard for all. The framework further adds that effective principals need to respect others and are respected by their school community. In Chapter 3 the principal highlighted the importance of school leaders being positive and enthusiastic. The principal displayed a positive and enthusiastic attitude through the following actions:

- being a role model, in particular in how he spoke to the children and the language he used; and
- being positive and respectful in his interactions with all members of the school community.

Furthermore, the school community was able to identify a number of leadership characteristics that would assist a school principal when cultivating a positive school culture. These qualities included:
- being approachable;
- being enthusiastic;
- being friendly; and
- being positive.

Developing relationships with all members of the school community

Chapter 2 established the importance of principals being able to facilitate positive and collaborative relationships, including managing conflict between people to restore positive relationships. The results of this research indicate the importance of the principal developing relationships with all members of the school community. Like a thread joining all the pieces to make a tapestry, relationships are crucial in linking all the aspects of a culture together. The principal developed relationships with all members of the school community and this was done by:
- placing a high importance upon student well-being and positive staff and student relationships. He was approachable and took time to listen;
- making personal connections with members of the school community; and
- attending all school events and therefore making himself accessible and visible.

Implementing procedures and policies that cultivate a positive culture

The findings of this research indicate that the principal was willing to implement many strategies that cultivated a positive culture. He was able to act upon his knowledge in regard to maintaining a positive school culture and implemented the following strategies:
- using positive language;
- modelling the behaviour that staff need to display, including taking time to build rapport with students;
- using a distributed leadership model by trusting his staff and not being too controlling or micromanaging;
- building relationships;
- reminding people of the school's vision and goals; and

- developing the team around you. The principal stated that he was always trying to build team culture by utilising the leadership skills of others, including the Heads of Departments and house coordinators.

> The principal needs to be flexible and encourage teamwork. You may have highly skilled individuals but it really is only a team approach that will provide success and deliver the best outcomes. (School Board Member 1)

4.4 The Key Actions Suggested by the School Community that Can Assist with the Cultivation of a Positive School Culture

This research has identified the actions by the school community that can assist with the cultivation of a positive school culture. These are presented in Figure 4.2.

Figure 4.2 Actions Suggested by the School Community that Contribute to a Positive Culture

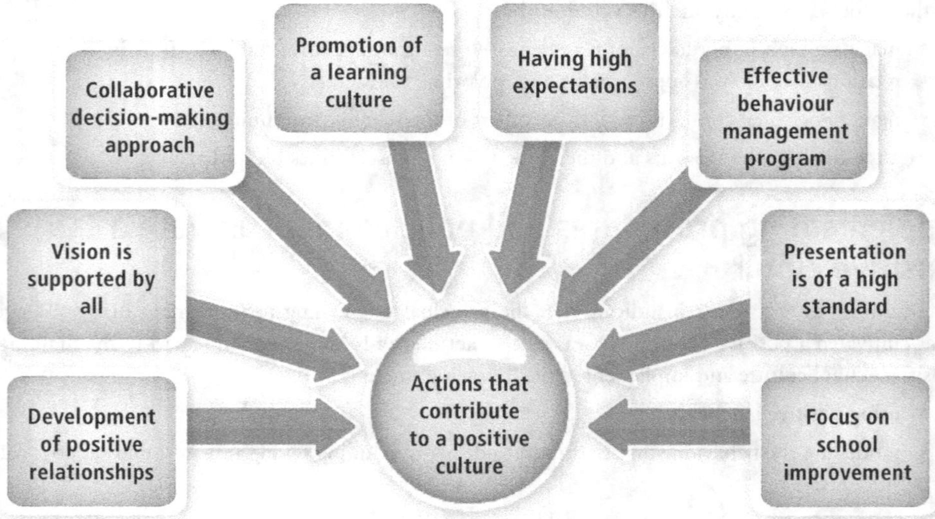

The actions contributing to a positive culture are:
- Collaborative decision-making approach
- Promotion of a learning culture
- Having high expectations
- Effective behaviour management program
- Vision is supported by all
- Presentation is of a high standard
- Development of positive relationships
- Focus on school improvement

The majority of actions in Figure 4.2 are consistent with those reported in the literature. However, this research has highlighted that a key requirement for the cultivation of a positive school culture is that the school community need to support the school's vision. Also, this research provides evidence

Chapter 4: Conclusions and Recommendations

of the link between the aesthetics of a school and the cultivation of a positive school culture that has not previously been documented.

The school vision is supported by all school community members

This research found that there was a high degree of collaboration between staff members to achieve shared goals. For the school community to support the school vision, the following actions were recommended by the school community:

- the vision and values of the school should be known to all;
- work together to achieve agreed goals. One Head of Department suggested that staff need to work together to achieve the vision or consider leaving the school;
- respectful relations must take place between all members of the school community; and
- the school communities must have a shared moral purpose.

Utilise a collaborative decision-making approach

As discussed in Chapter 3, the principal was a strong advocate for a distributed leadership approach. This outcome is consistent with the supporting behaviour in the ACGCEO (2009) leadership framework that states principals need to actively listen to the views of others. A collaborative decision-making approach was fostered in this research school by the following actions:

- allowing staff and students to have input into things that directly impact on them;
- ensuring there are effective communication procedures; and
- distributing the leadership responsibilities among staff, parents and students.

Promotion of a professional learning culture

The promotion of a professional learning culture in the research school has strong links with the following supporting behaviour presented in Chapter 2 – namely, *engages in workplace learning and relevant professional development.*

To promote a positive culture, the school community suggested the following actions:

- encourage the professional development of individual staff;
- have staff work in collaboration;
- encourage innovation and programs to meet the needs of all students. In the survey, the school community indicated that the programs and extra-curricular activities were aspects that were great about the school; and
- make student and teacher learning a high priority.

If you have a positive culture, then learning is so much better. Positivity makes things work better. If it is negative no one is happy, no one wants to be there and no one wants to be with negative people, so no one learns as people just switch off. (Head of Department 2)

The school implements an effective behaviour management program

The school had a number of procedures and expectations that fostered an effective behaviour management program that included:

- students continuously being reminded of the expectations and the values of the school. This was evident in the survey that the principal would often speak to the school community about expectations and values;
- teachers focused on teaching. The principal spoke about the need for creating a learning culture and the importance of teachers improving their skills; and
- there was a consistent approach to behaviour management and expectations.

Development of positive relationships

An important aspect of a positive school culture is the quality of relationships between all members within the school. The development of positive relationships was promoted by the following actions:

- treating people with respect. This was viewed by the school community as a core value;
- providing a positive classroom/work environment. This was viewed as important by teachers as they believed a positive classroom environment produced better student results;
- ensuring people felt valued. Staff and students reported they felt valued when the principal listened to them; and
- acknowledging people for their efforts. An example of this was when the principal congratulated students at assembly.

A focus on school improvement

The results from this research have shown that the staff were encouraged to provide quality programs to facilitate school improvement, and the school focused on this by:

- creating a positive school culture. The principal emphasised the importance of his staff using positive language;
- supporting staff when leading activities and initiatives. The principal would try and attend all school events;
- making learning a high priority. The principal would visit the classrooms and join in the lessons, including trying to speak French; and
- having a team approach to achieving the school's goals. To achieve this the principal tried to develop the capabilities of the leadership team.

Ensure school presentation is of a high standard
Results from the research indicated that the presentation of the grounds was a strong indicator of a positive school culture and the appearance was enhanced by the following actions:
- the front office staff are welcoming and the office has displays of children's work;
- the grounds are well maintained; and
- ensuring that the school was physically attractive.

4.5 Recommendations for the Cultivation and Maintenance of a Positive School Culture

This section presents a number of recommendations that could help principals improve the culture within their school. The recommendations that follow have drawn on the available literature, the results from this research, the previous discussion and this researcher's personal experience working as a school principal.

Recommendations for principals

The following recommendations for school principals are based on the key findings of this research, and also draw upon the literature reviewed in Chapter 3.

Recommendation 1: The principal needs to first examine the school's existing culture before seeking to change the culture

This recommendation is consistent with the literature findings which emphasised the importance of evaluating the culture of the school before making changes. In Chapter 3, the principal recommended that school leaders have a clear picture of what is happening currently at the school and compare the existing culture to the vision of the school. The following are actions that can assist principals when examining the existing school culture:
- collect data to explore what is working and what needs to be addressed;
- listen to the school community about concerns; and
- visit classrooms and attend school events.

Recommendation 2: The principal needs to articulate a shared vision with the school community

The principal's ability to communicate to the various stakeholders the school's vision and goals was seen as a strength by the school community in this research. The results from this case study have shown that the principal articulated a shared vision to the school community in a number of ways, and this can be done by:

- establishing clear guidelines so that staff know what behaviours are expected;
- being a role model in carrying out the values in daily routines and interactions;
- communicating the principles and values that are going to assist the school to move forward at every opportunity; *and*
- ensuring that staff align their behaviour to what the school's vision and goals are.

Recommendation 3: The principal needs to make the cultivation of a positive school culture a priority

The principal felt that the key role of school leadership was cultivating a school culture that promoted learning so that student outcomes improve. He believed that an important aspect of his role was to lead the learning and therefore was active with his own learning. This result aligns with the following observation from ACGCEO (2009, p. 5), "There is no documented case of a school successfully turning itself around and lifting student achievement in the absence of talented school leadership." The above recommendation was actioned by the principal in the following ways:

- making the cultivation of a positive school culture a priority;
- valuing and acknowledging others; and
- creating a positive message by using positive language.

Recommendation 4: Principals need to be visible, approachable and available for all members of the school community

The research has demonstrated the importance of the principal being not only visible but available to all members of the community. As shown in this research, the principal can utilise the following strategies to connect with the school community:

- visiting classrooms daily, walking around the school and talking to the students;
- attending all school activities; and
- ensuring that one member of the leadership team is present at school events.

Recommendation 5: Principal needs to remain positive and enthusiastic

In Chapter 3, the respondents in the interviews and focus groups stressed the important role the principal has in the development of a positive school culture, with the school community suggesting that the principal sets the tone and standards for the whole school. The principal influenced the school community through his words and actions, and displayed positivity and enthusiasm in the following ways:

- using positive language and being friendly;
- modelling the behaviour he wanted staff to display; and
- celebrating achievements by publicly acknowledging people's efforts.

Recommendation 6: Principals need to build relationships with all members of the school community

An outcome of this research, discussed in Chapter 3, was the importance of building relationships in maintaining a positive culture. This result is consistent with that reported in the literature review. Positive relationships were seen as important, as they are the lubricant that lessened the friction between the various parts of the organisation. Therefore, they provide greater efficiency for the school to move forward. Specifically, the school community suggested that the principal use the following strategies to build relationships with others:

- being approachable and friendly;
- being caring and supportive;
- treating others with respect; and
- visiting the classrooms and attending school events.

> *I really enjoy my job, I love it. I love the interaction with the other staff and the students. I enjoy all aspects.*
> (Teacher Assistant 2)

Recommendation 7: Principals need to know how to enhance school performance

The results from the research found that the principal modelled the behaviour he wanted from his staff and that they were able to implement what he suggested. A finding from this research is that one of the principal's major tasks is encouraging all members of the school community to work together to achieve the school's goals. The principal can action this recommendation by:

- ensuring the expectations and goals of the school are well known;
- removing obstacles that reduce teachers' ability to focus upon teaching; and
- encouraging staff to examine data to ensure new programs or procedures are fulfilling goals and expectations.

Recommendation 8: The school needs to recruit quality staff who can support the vision of the school

It is evident from this research and the literature that teacher quality has a significant influence on student performance and motivation. This research also revealed that attracting quality staff to the school is an ongoing issue not only for this research school but for many regional and remote schools in Australia. The principal used the following actions to attract quality staff:

- providing a positive workplace environment;
- developing a supportive leadership team;
- providing an effective behaviour management program; and
- hiring staff that would accept and support the school's vision and existing expectations.

Recommendations for members of school community to cultivate a positive school culture

The cultivation and maintenance of a positive school culture requires input from all members of the school community. Therefore, the following recommendations could be actioned by members of the school community to improve the culture within their school.

Recommendation 9: All members of the school community need to know and support a shared vision of the school

The school community felt that an important element of the school's positive culture was the underlying values that permeated through their interactions with each other. The school was able to have a shared vision by:

- school leaders repeating the vision in a variety of ways to all members of the school;
- having a set of principles, philosophies and values; and
- school community members modelling behaviour, values and expectations.

Recommendation 10: The school encourages all members of the school community to contribute to decision making

The results of the research presented in Chapter 3 indicate the need to allow others an opportunity to contribute to the decision making of the school, and that it should not be dependent on one person. This finding is consistent with results reported in the literature, and in this research it was found that the staff, students and parents wanted to be listened to and have input into aspects of the school. A collaborative approach to decision making was facilitated through the following actions:

- encouraging parent groups to be actively involved with school activities;
- ensuring collaborative practices are promoted; and
- seeking the contribution of all members of the school community.

Recommendation 11: The school promotes a professional learning culture

The findings of this research revealed that the principal's awareness of best teaching practices enabled him to lead the school in professional learning. In this respect, the AITSL (2012) suggests that collaboration has a powerful effect in magnifying the benefits of professional learning and supports the learning undertaken by individuals. This recommendation relates to one part of the school community – the staff. A school can promote a professional learning culture by:

- encouraging staff to attend professional development;
- having the leadership team actively engaged in learning;
- organising time so that staff can plan together; and
- having a strong focus on teaching and learning.

Chapter 4: Conclusions and Recommendations

Recommendation 12: The school implements an effective behaviour management program

This research has highlighted the importance of schools implementing an effective behaviour management program. This was evidenced by students using good manners, showing respect and following school rules. In this research, the school had an effective implementation of a behaviour management program by:

- having a leadership team member address issues with students;
- students having clear boundaries and expectations of behaviour; and
- having clear guidelines that are consistently applied by staff.

Recommendation 13: The school has a continuous focus on school improvement

As considered previously, this school had a deliberate focus on continuous school improvement by adopting the following strategies:

- making student learning and teacher standards a high priority;
- up-skilling staff by providing professional development opportunities; and
- developing a shared approach to achieve the school's goals.

Recommendation 14: The school ensures the presentation of the grounds and facilities are of a high standard

It was discussed in Chapter 3 how the presentation of the school grounds was an indicator as to whether or not the school had a positive school culture. The parents suggested that the physical environment also plays a part in the cultivation of a positive school culture and they were appreciative of the well-maintained grounds. This recommendation can be achieved by the following actions:

- having the school grounds be well maintained;
- celebrating the students' achievements by having honour boards and the work of the students on display; and
- displaying religious symbols or artefacts around the school as a visible reminder to the school community of what is considered important.

I think the school is beautiful. The grounds here are absolutely stunning. You drive past here and look at the place and say "wow". (Teacher)

Reflective questions

- What are the most useful recommendations for your situation?
- Which of the key actions for school leaders to cultivate a positive culture do you need to prioritise?

Decisive actions
- List some of the comments made by the school community that resonated with you.
- Take time each day to walk through the school and look for the good in the students and staff by acknowledging their efforts.
- Positive relationship building is an excellent tool for leaders to utilise to increase their organisation's ability to develop and achieve their best outcomes. Ensure you visit the staff room during breaks to stay connected with your community.
- Write down some personal goals that will assist you in cultivating a positive school culture.
- Leadership can be both rewarding and stressful. To cultivate a positive culture, leaders need to radiate positivity. Explore ways that enhance all facets of your life so that you can start work energised. Remember to take care of yourself so you can inspire others.

4.6 Concluding Remarks

This book has presented a comprehensive study exploring the role of the school principal in the cultivation of a positive school culture. It was found that the cultivation of a positive school culture is the combination of the school community working for the collective good to achieve the goals of the school. It was also demonstrated that positive relationships between members of the school do facilitate the cultivation of a positive school culture. This book has revealed the potential benefits of cultivating a positive school culture. It has also provided practical strategies for school principals to improve the culture at their own school.

In this research, it was shown that the principal was able to cultivate a positive school culture because his personal virtues allowed him to model the behaviour that reflected the school's values and mission statement, and he then encouraged others in the school community to do the same. In this respect, the results revealed that the principal had implemented many of the core capabilities and supporting behaviours as presented in the ACGCEO (2009) leadership framework and as such demonstrated that he was a highly competent school leader.

Principals need to ensure that they are positive themselves as they are the major influence on the culture of a school. For an education system to make substantial improvements, the cultivation of a positive culture in each school needs to be a high priority to ensure that all staff have high expectations. It would appear that, from this research, how successful the school is depends on the principal's ability to unite the school community in working together to achieve the school's goals and vision. Hopefully the research will stimulate others to adopt the recommendations presented in this chapter and serve as a springboard for further research.

Chapter 5

The Positive School Culture Improvement Tool

5.1 Introduction

This chapter presents an audit tool for principals to review and analyse their efforts to cultivate a positive culture within their own school. The Positive School Culture Improvement Tool consists of eleven key themes: 1) vision/mission/values; 2) curriculum; 3) students; 4) leadership; 5) teaching and learning; 6) building community; 7) communication and conflict resolution; 8) artefacts and physical environment; 9) staff; 10) events/celebrations/traditions and 11) perceptions/thinking/feeling. The tool utilises the recommendations from the school community and the strategies the principal was already implementing in maintaining and improving the positive school culture. There are 275 strategies in the tool! Readers will have the opportunity to examine their own current practice by using the recommendations as indicators when auditing their school culture. The tool has been created for school leaders to assist them in their own school improvement plans and in creating cultures of high expectations. The tool is intended to provide school principals with many practical strategies to assist them in cultivating a positive culture at their own schools.

Pfeffer and Sutton (2000) advocate the principle of *kaizen* – the need for change to promote continuous improvement, with most of the changes being small and simple. Pfeffer and Sutton (2000, p. 11) remark, "Time after time, people understand the issues, understand what needs to happen to affect performance, but don't do the things they know they should." The following audit tool is an example of the research school implementing many small actions to create a positive school culture. Principals will need to be discerning as to which strategies they utilise at their own school to cultivate a positive school culture. When examining their own school culture, principals may like to use the tool by applying the following Likert key to each strategy: Please answer all statements by ticking the most appropriate number. (Scoring: 1 = Never; 2 = Rarely; 3 = Sometimes; 4 = Often; 5 = Always).

Table 5.1 Theme 1 – Vision/Mission/Values

(Scoring: 1 = Never; 2 = Rarely; 3 = Sometimes; 4 = Often; 5 = Always)

The research respondents suggested the following strategies that the school principal used or could use to cultivate a positive school culture.	1	2	3	4	5
1. Apprises staff and students of high expectations					
2. There is continual sense of striving to improve					
3. Leadership team have integrity in all dealings					
4. Staff participate in long-term planning					
5. Regularly reminds people of the school's core values					
6. Mission statement is often mentioned					
7. Principal lives out the vision himself					
8. The core values of the school are stated regularly					
9. School's vision and values are displayed					
10. Staff have a shared moral purpose					
11. Give staff direction so they know what to focus on					
12. Help staff and students set goals and achieve their personal best					
13. Encourage everyone to contribute to improving the school					
14. Staff take responsibility for school performance					
15. Insist on high expectations of staff to go that extra mile					
16. Goals of school are often mentioned to parents and students					
17. Positive, friendly environment is provided					
18. Principal articulates clearly the direction of the school					
19. Students are explicitly taught values					
20. Principal maintains personal values					
21. Respectful relationships and responsibility are clearly evident					
22. Principal's actions are aligned and consistent with the school's vision					
23. There is a visible school development plan					
24. Has shared goals with all staff and departments and parents					
25. Principal has a clear vision that is shared with the community					

Table 5.2 Theme 2 – Curriculum

(Scoring: 1 = Never; 2 = Rarely; 3 = Sometimes; 4 = Often; 5 = Always)

The research respondents suggested the following strategies that the school principal used or could use to cultivate a positive school culture	1	2	3	4	5
1. Provide an interesting, relevant curriculum					
2. Offer a wide range of extra-curricular activities					
3. Large variety of subjects from which to choose					
4. Whole-team approach to implementing the curriculum effectively					
5. Acknowledgement of achievements made with changes to curriculum					
6. Have a number of signature programs in the school in which school is outstanding					
7. Teachers are given time to write up curriculum programs					
8. Time is given to implement changes					
9. Students to have an understanding of the social issues that are current					
10. Offer a variety of specialist subjects					
11. Provide current and engaging units that are of high quality					
12. Ensure cultural and sporting programs are of a high standard					
13. Encourage a sense of belonging through the arts program and through playing a team sport					
14. School provides learning activities that motivate the students					
15. Curriculum promotes the holistic development of students					
16. Provide many cultural opportunities					
17. Encourage retreats, excursions and social outings among students					
18. Keep up to date on the latest educational trends					
19. Professional development is supported					
20. Ensure teachers are teaching in areas in which they are trained					
21. Curriculum activities cater for the diverse range of student abilities and interests					
22. Implement change or modify programs to improve outcomes					
23. Ensure staff have time to plan together					
24. Analyse data and results of programs that are being used to know what is working					
25. Provide a co-curriculum program that essentially gives every kid a chance to succeed and have a sense of belonging					

Table 5.3 Theme 3 – Students

(Scoring: 1 = Never; 2 = Rarely; 3 = Sometimes; 4 = Often; 5 = Always)

The research respondents suggested the following strategies that the school principal used or could use to cultivate a positive school culture.	1	2	3	4	5
1. Principal and staff have positive relationships with students					
2. Promote inclusivity of students with disabilities and their needs are met					
3. Principal regularly engages in conversations with students					
4. Provide good learning support in classrooms					
5. Give students opportunities to support others in need					
6. Respectful relationships exist between staff and students					
7. Give students the flexibility to make choices, avoid mandating subjects					
8. Generate leadership roles for students					
9. Ensure staff use positive language to all the students					
10. Ensure students have a great sense of belonging					
11. Students display school values and expectations					
12. Students are praised often					
13. Allow students to produce work in a variety of ways to cater for all learning styles					
14. Staff mix with students at recess and lunchtimes					
15. Focus on student improvement so that teachers modify the learning process to get better results					
16. Have high expectations of students' manners and behaviour					
17. Students are encouraged to do their best					
18. Pastoral care and student well-being are viewed as important					
19. Teachers are fair and look for the good in each student					
20. Focus on raising students' self-esteem					
21. Encourage the students to be compassionate and caring					
22. Students are listened to and contribute to decision making					
23. The students are valued, as are their opinions					
24. Give the students lots of opportunities to organise things like committees and clubs					
25. Encourage the students to be active at lunchtimes					

Table 5.4 Theme 4 – Leadership

(Scoring: 1 = Never; 2 = Rarely; 3 = Sometimes; 4 = Often; 5 = Always)

The research respondents suggested the following strategies that the school principal used or could use to cultivate a positive school culture.	1	2	3	4	5
1. Principal is genuinely interested in all areas of the school					
2. Principal is viewed as a competent, credible teacher					
3. Models expectations					
4. There is always a member of the leadership team present at a school activity					
5. Keeps working on the school's culture the whole time					
6. Principal is conscious of every child's situation and circumstances					
7. Implements the procedures, policies and leadership structures that are not dependent on the principal					
8. Walks around the school, talks to the students and is highly visible					
9. Principal follows through on what they say they are going to do					
10. Is highly organised					
11. Encourages the students and uses praise often					
12. Visits classrooms regularly and talks to students and teachers					
13. Principal is willing to go the extra mile for students and staff					
14. Principal acknowledges everyone with a friendly greeting					
15. Principal is actively involved with school activities					
16. Provides constructive/positive feedback					
17. Displays courage and confidence when making difficult decisions					
18. Be willing to engage with the parents and listen – is consultative					
19. Involves others in decision-making process – collaborative approach					
20. The principal regularly thanks staff and keeps reinforcing that message of gratitude					
21. Is viewed as a leader of learning, an instructional leader					
22. Is able to unite staff to work together to deliver quality outcomes					
23. Leadership team is supportive and shows compassion					
24. Displays servant leadership and allows people to contribute					
25. Uses the distributed leadership model					

Table 5.5 Theme 5 – Teaching and learning

(Scoring: 1 = Never; 2 = Rarely; 3 = Sometimes; 4 = Often; 5 = Always)

The research respondents suggested the following strategies that the school principal used or could use to cultivate a positive school culture.	1	2	3	4	5
1. Keep the focus on the students and their learning					
2. Be very supportive of staff endeavours					
3. Ensure all teachers are trained in what they are teaching					
4. Provide opportunities for people to work together					
5. Keep trying to improve teaching standards					
6. Promote a culture in the school that students are expected to learn					
7. Provide free tutoring for maths, English and science after school					
8. Have high expectations of students' achievement					
9. Financially support staff to attend professional development					
10. Embrace teachers as leaders					
11. Students take responsibility for their learning					
12. Ensure staff have the skills to cater for diverse needs of students					
13. Provide clear learning guidelines for students					
14. Teachers take on added responsibilities willingly					
15. Principal regularly visits classrooms and talks to students and teachers					
16. Principal shows students that they care and respect them					
17. Minimise administrative tasks so teachers are able to concentrate their energy on what is important – student learning					
18. Promote academic rigour					
19. Support new innovations for learning and self-development					
20. Strive for excellence in teaching and providing a safe and stimulating environment					
21. Provide clear, consistent classroom boundaries/expectations					
22. Encourage a strong focus on academic improvement					
23. Promote a positive learning environment in classrooms					
24. Provide new teachers with mentors					
25. Encourage networking, and staff working and learning together to create a learning culture					

Chapter 5: The Positive School Culture Improvement Tool

Table 5.6 Theme 6 – Building community

(Scoring: 1 = Never; 2 = Rarely; 3 = Sometimes; 4 = Often; 5 = Always)

The research respondents suggested the following strategies that the school principal used or could use to cultivate a positive school culture.	1	2	3	4	5
1. Office staff are friendly, personable and greet people with a smile					
2. The school's prospectus and web page looks professional and creates a positive image to show the wider community					
3. Visitors offered a tea, coffee or water					
4. Principal goes out of his way to speak to parents about their child					
5. Support families who are struggling and offer assistance					
6. Principal has shared goals with all staff, departments and parents					
7. Principal makes a point of coming into the staffroom at lunch and takes time to know staff and students					
8. Provide opportunities for students to do community service					
9. Spend time with school captains					
10. Takes time to develop good working relationships					
11. Is approachable and accessible by walking around the grounds before and after school					
12. Support Parents & Friends, and school board, by attending meetings					
13. Consult with parents, students and staff when deciding things					
14. Encourage parent involvement through activities like awards nights, swimming carnivals, tuck shop and parent/teacher interviews					
15. Take time to build relationships with members of school community					
16. Promote house group structure where staff have connection with students					
17. Develop a strong 'post' school affiliation					
18. Actively engage in conversation with all staff					
19. Encourage community involvement within the school					
20. Utilise personnel from head office					
21. Attends all sports carnivals and school activities					
22. Develop a high level of trust among the staff					
23. Acknowledge everyone's contribution to making the school better					
24. Support activities that promote a sense of belonging					
25. Know parents and their children by name					

Table 5.7 Theme 7 – Communication and conflict resolution

(Scoring: 1 = Never; 2 = Rarely; 3 = Sometimes; 4 = Often; 5 = Always)

The research respondents suggested the following strategies that the school principal used or could use to cultivate a positive school culture.	1	2	3	4	5
1. Create a positive message by using positive language					
2. Be a highly accomplished public speaker					
3. Explain reasons for changes					
4. Principal is accessible, available and approachable					
5. Encourage teacher/parent feedback					
6. Thank people for things at morning meetings					
7. School board and staff are involved in decision making					
8. Principal is enthusiastic and displays an optimistic attitude					
9. School community is consulted about long-term goals					
10. Remain calm even when dealing with significant issues					
11. Use a variety of communication methods to keep parents informed					
12. Address issues with dignity, sensitivity and confidence					
13. Provide an informative newsletter					
14. Regularly call parents in regard to positive feedback about their child					
15. Be unfailingly positive and affirming					
16. Be slow in aggravation, but lavish in praise					
17. Make time for others and display genuine care and support					
18. The school guidelines, procedures and rules are consistently applied					
19. Staff are consistent when implementing the behaviour management program					
20. Communicate principles that are going to help the school move forward at every opportunity					
21. There are clear and firm boundaries and rules					
22. Leadership and staff are polite and respectful to all students					
23. Zero tolerance for bullying by teachers and students alike					
24. Keep staff well informed about what is happening					
25. Ensure staff are accessible for parents to discuss queries					

Chapter 5: The Positive School Culture Improvement Tool

Table 5.8 Theme 8 – Artefacts and physical environment

(Scoring: 1 = Never; 2 = Rarely; 3 = Sometimes; 4 = Often; 5 = Always)

The research respondents suggested the following strategies that the school principal used or could use to cultivate a positive school culture.	1	2	3	4	5
1. There are plants, fish tanks, seats in the foyer					
2. Things of beauty in the school like landscape gardens and artwork					
3. Overall appearance of the school is very high					
4. School is well resourced					
5. Memorial plaques for any students who die					
6. School values and mission statement are displayed					
7. Prominent displays of acknowledgment of people who have impacted upon the school					
8. The school is visually appealing from the street					
9. The school crest and motto are highly visible					
10. There are quiet areas for students to go to					
11. Well-maintained grounds and buildings					
12. Clean and tidy facilities					
13. Front office displays of student work					
14. Adequate seating is provided					
15. Maintain the honour board in the office foyer					
16. Keep upgrading school facilities, especially in the area of technology					
17. High standard of dress code maintained					
18. Provide efficient and quality tuck shop facility					
19. Banners and flags are highly visible					
20. Visible symbols clearly state what is viewed as important					
21. Cultural and sporting achievements are on display					
22. Toilet facilities are of a high standard and are light and open					
23. Academic awards and trophies are prominently displayed					
24. There are positive quotes around the school					
25. School rules and expectations are displayed					

Table 5.9 Theme 9 – Staff

(Scoring: 1 = Never; 2 = Rarely; 3 = Sometimes; 4 = Often; 5 = Always)

The research respondents suggested the following strategies that the school principal used or could use to cultivate a positive school culture.	1	2	3	4	5
1. Keep improving your people so everyone is moving forward					
2. Build a relationship with each staff member					
3. Continual team-building processes so the culture is resilient when people leave					
4. Ensure the people you select are able to do the role					
5. Know each staff member's strengths and utilise these					
6. Attract positive, quality staff					
7. Have an expectation that staff work collaboratively					
8. Surround yourself with intelligent, positive, capable people					
9. Create a dynamic, unified, positive team					
10. Develop good rapport with each staff member					
11. Treat and value each staff member regardless of their role					
12. Focus on team building					
13. Provide a cake or coffee occasionally to acknowledge staff who have willingly done something extra					
14. Display respect for each person					
15. Encourage staff that are working together and sharing ideas					
16. Encourage positive relationships between staff and students					
17. Allow staff to enjoy changes before moving on					
18. Empower staff to lead					
19. Expect staff to be positive and enthusiastic toward each other and students					
20. Put support structures in place for new teachers					
21. Staff treated fairly and with respect					
22. Ensure all members of the leadership team are working closely with each other					
23. Keep encouraging and developing a team approach					
24. Support staff, especially when they are experiencing issues					
25. Office staff are positive and helpful to every inquiry					

Table 5.10 Theme 10 – Events/Celebrations/Traditions

(Scoring: 1 = Never; 2 = Rarely; 3 = Sometimes; 4 = Often; 5 = Always)

The research respondents suggested the following strategies that the school principal used or could use to cultivate a positive school culture.	1	2	3	4	5
1. All members of school community are encouraged to contribute					
2. Encourage sporting/cultural activities					
3. Cater for students' social needs					
4. Recognise and celebrate past traditions					
5. Provide activities that promote a sense of belonging					
6. Whole-school approach to behaviour management					
7. Focus on excellence in scholastic pursuits					
8. Leadership team member at each student activity					
9. Principal provides a positive message at assemblies					
10. Achievement is recognised and celebrated					
11. People who have shaped the school are often recognised and their stories shared					
12. High expectations are consistently applied and rewarded					
13. Provide different clubs at lunchtime and after school					
14. Students are all encouraged to participate in all school events					
15. Continue with the various award nights and cultural nights					
16. Encouraging social events in departments and after school					
17. Have a well-organised administration so the school runs smoothly					
18. Have house co-ordinators organise activities and events for the students					
19. Opportunities for students to perform and represent the school					
20. Encourage important school rituals during homeroom					
21. Acknowledge extra staff effort with a bottle of wine or a coffee					
22. Students can go to a variety of areas during breaks					
23. Have consistent daily routines					
24. Principal actively participates in activities					
25. Display students' work					

Table 5.11 Theme 11 – Perceptions/Thinking/Feeling

(Scoring: 1 = Never; 2 = Rarely; 3 = Sometimes; 4 = Often; 5 = Always)

The research respondents suggested the following strategies that the school principal used or could use to cultivate a positive school culture.	1	2	3	4	5
1. Staff feel valued and supported by leadership team and parents					
2. A safe environment is provided					
3. Everyone treats each other with respect					
4. Principal is seen as happy, friendly and positive					
5. Teachers provide a positive classroom environment					
6. Staff have a healthy understanding of what is a collaborative culture					
7. The principal is always thanking staff and keeps reinforcing that message of gratitude					
8. People feel supported and appreciated					
9. There is a friendly, positive atmosphere					
10. Search for qualities in people and utilise these for betterment of school					
11. Principal is seen as a role model who has integrity					
12. Teachers are viewed as dedicated, professional and caring					
13. Everyone knows the expectations through the leadership team modelling them					
14. Principal is seen as a visionary leader who has expertise in education					
15. Principal always gives 100% effort					
16. Principal looks for what is right in a situation or person					
17. The principal is seen as passionate about the school and the students					
18. Enforce rules fairly and consistently					
19. Effective behaviour management program is consistently implemented					
20. Ensure that all staff and teachers follow policies and procedures					
21. Leadership team are open to new ideas					
22. Continued belief that all children can learn					
23. Be supportive of all students					
24. Inspire others to be the best that they can be					
25. Encourage school spirit through the house system					

Chapter 5: The Positive School Culture Improvement Tool

5.2 Summary

This chapter presented many different strategies that the school community recommended would assist in the cultivation of a positive school culture. Most of the strategies listed were already being applied by the principal. The principal is clearly implementing many small actions that are collectively producing a positive culture. The Positive Culture Improvement Tool provides a deep insight into how a school community, in particular a school principal, cultivates a positive school culture to enhance organisational performance. Some of the strategies were given higher priority than others by the principal. School principals would need to examine their own school culture and apply those that would be most appropriate to their own school situation.

Appendices

Appendix A: School culture survey for staff

(Scoring: 1 = Never; 2 = Rarely; 3 = Sometimes; 4 = Often; 5 = Always)

Instructions – Please answer all questions by ticking the most appropriate number. There are no right or wrong answers.	1	2	3	4	5
Vision/Mission/Values					
1. The principal talks to staff about the school's expectations					
2. Our school's values guide our daily actions at school					
3. The principal has a clear vision that is shared with the community					
4. Staff have a shared moral purpose of high expectations for all students					
5. The school's vision and values are displayed					
Curriculum					
6. Staff are encouraged to provide innovative programs					
7. Curriculum activities cater for the diverse range of student abilities and interests					
8. The school provides many extra-curricular activities					
9. The school offers a wide selection of subjects					
10. There is a whole-team approach to implementing the curriculum effectively					
Students					
11. Students at this school are generally well-behaved					
12. All students are expected to achieve success					
13. Students like coming to school					
14. Students' well-being is important					
15. Respectful relationships exist between staff and students					
Leadership					
16. The principal has a positive attitude					
17. The principal unites staff to work together to achieve school goals					
18. The principal involves staff in the decision making of the school					
19. The principal attends school activities					
20. The principal gives a high priority to building positive relationships with staff					
21. The principal provides effective leadership					

REPRODUCIBLE

Positive School Culture and Effective Leadership

Instructions – Please answer all questions by ticking the most appropriate number. There are no right or wrong answers.	1	2	3	4	5
Teaching and learning					
22. Professional development is encouraged at this school					
23. The school places a high priority on improving teaching standards					
24. A positive learning environment is provided in classrooms					
25. Opportunities for people to work together are provided					
26. The staff have high expectations of all students to learn					
Building community					
27. Parents provide strong community support					
28. There is a friendly school community at this school					
29. People at this school treat each other with respect					
30. Staff have a sense of belonging to the school					
31. There is a high level of trust among students and staff					
Communication and conflict resolution					
32. Staff are treated fairly at the school					
33. The students learn to handle conflict respectfully					
34. Staff keep parents informed about their child's progress					
35. Staff are well informed about what is happening					
36. The school guidelines, procedures and rules are consistently applied					
Staff					
37. I enjoy coming to work					
38. Staff are provided with leadership opportunities					
39. Staff show a willingness to implement change to improve learning					
40. Staff at this school are enthusiastic					
41. There is an expectation that staff work collaboratively					
Events/Celebrations/Traditions					
42. Our school has traditions and rituals that are celebrated					
43. We have special events and customs that distinguish us as a school					
44. Achievement is recognised and celebrated					
45. All members of the school community are encouraged to contribute					
46. There are opportunities for students to perform and represent the school					

REPRODUCIBLE

Appendix A: School Culture Survey for Staff

Instructions – Please answer all questions by ticking the most appropriate number. There are no right or wrong answers.	1	2	3	4	5
Artefacts and physical environment					
47. Cultural and sporting achievements are on display					
48. The school provides an attractive physical environment					
49. There are visible symbols that clearly state what is viewed as important					
50. The facilities are clean and tidy					
Perceptions/Thinking/Feeling					
51. This is a caring school					
52. The school has a positive work environment					
53. Staff are always working on ways to improve student outcomes					
54. Staff feel appreciated for the work they do					
55. Staff encourage students to achieve their personal best					

56. What aspects of the school are great?

57. Can you list three things that you would like to happen that are not currently happening at the school?

Thank you for your time in completing this survey.

REPRODUCIBLE

Appendix B: School culture survey for parents

(Scoring: 1 = Never; 2 = Rarely; 3 = Sometimes; 4 = Often; 5 = Always)

Instructions – Please answer all questions by ticking the most appropriate number. There are no right or wrong answers.	1	2	3	4	5
Vision/Mission/Values					
1. The principal talks to parents about the school's expectations					
2. Our school's values guide the daily actions of the school					
3. The principal has a clear vision that is shared with the community					
4. Staff have a shared moral purpose of high expectations for all students					
5. The school's vision and values are displayed					
Curriculum					
6. The school provides innovative programs					
7. Curriculum activities cater for the diverse range of student abilities and interests					
8. The school provides many extra-curricular activities					
9. The school offers a wide selection of subjects					
10. There is a whole-school approach to implementing the curriculum effectively					
Students					
11. Students at this school are generally well-behaved					
12. My child is expected to achieve success					
13. My child likes coming to school					
14. Students' well-being is important					
15. Respectful relationships exist between staff and students					
Leadership					
16. The principal has a positive attitude					
17. The principal unites the school community to work together to achieve school goals					
18. The principal involves parents in the decision making of the school					
19. The principal attends school activities					
20. The principal gives a high priority to building positive relationships with staff					
21. The principal provides effective leadership					

REPRODUCIBLE

Positive School Culture and Effective Leadership

Instructions – Please answer all questions by ticking the most appropriate number. There are no right or wrong answers.	1	2	3	4	5
Teaching and learning					
22. Professional development is encouraged at this school					
23. The school places a high priority on improving teaching standards					
24. A positive learning environment is provided in the classrooms					
25. Opportunities for the community to work together are provided					
26. The staff have high expectations for my child to learn					
Building community					
27. Parents provide strong community support					
28. There is a friendly school community at this school					
29. People at this school treat each other with respect					
30. My child has a sense of belonging to the school					
31. My child has a high level of trust toward staff					
Communication and conflict resolution					
32. My child is treated fairly at the school					
33. The students learn to handle conflict respectfully					
34. Staff keep me informed about my child's progress					
35. Parents are well informed about what is happening					
36. The school guidelines, procedures and rules are consistently applied					
Staff					
37. Staff seem positive in their roles					
38. Staff take on various leadership roles					
39. Staff show a willingness to improve my child's learning					
40. Staff at this school are enthusiastic					
41. Staff work collaboratively					
Events/Celebrations/Traditions					
42. The school has traditions and rituals that are celebrated					
43. The school has special events and customs that distinguish it as a school					
44. Achievement is recognised and celebrated					
45. All members of the school community are encouraged to contribute					
46. There are opportunities for students to perform and represent the school					

REPRODUCIBLE

Appendix B: School Culture Survey for Parents

Instructions – Please answer all questions by ticking the most appropriate number. There are no right or wrong answers.	1	2	3	4	5
Artefacts and physical environment					
47. Cultural and sporting achievements are on display					
48. The school provides an attractive physical environment					
49. There are visible symbols that clearly state what is viewed as important					
50. The facilities are clean and tidy					
Perceptions/Thinking/Feeling					
51. This is a caring school					
52. The school provides a positive work environment for my child					
53. Staff are always working on ways to improve student outcomes					
54. My child feels valued by staff					
55. Staff encourage students to achieve their personal best					

56. What aspects of your school are great?

57. Can you list three things that you would like to happen that are not currently happening at the school?

Thank you for your time in completing this survey.

REPRODUCIBLE

Appendix C: School culture survey for students

(Scoring: 1 = Never; 2 = Rarely; 3 = Sometimes; 4 = Often; 5 = Always)

Instructions – Please answer all questions by ticking the most appropriate number. There are no right or wrong answers.	1	2	3	4	5
Vision/Mission/Values					
1. The principal talks to the students about the school's expectations					
2. Our school's values guide my daily actions at the school					
3. The principal has a clear vision that is shared with the students					
4. Staff have high expectations for all students					
5. The school's vision and values are displayed					
Curriculum					
6. The school provides innovative programs					
7. Curriculum activities cater for the diverse range of students' abilities and interests					
8. The school provides many extra-curricular activities					
9. The school offers a wide selection of subjects					
10. The staff work together to teach the curriculum effectively					
Students					
11. Students at this school are generally well-behaved					
12. The staff expect me to achieve success					
13. I like coming to school					
14. The staff are concerned about how I am feeling					
15. Respectful relationships exist between staff and students					
Leadership					
16. The principal has a positive attitude					
17. The principal unites everyone to work together to achieve school goals					
18. The principal involves students in the decision making of the school					
19. The principal attends school activities					
20. The principal takes time to build positive relationships with students					
21. The principal is an excellent leader					

REPRODUCIBLE

Positive School Culture and Effective Leadership

Instructions – Please answer all questions by ticking the most appropriate number. There are no right or wrong answers.	1	2	3	4	5
Teaching and learning					
22. Teachers teach the subjects that they are trained for					
23. The teaching standards are very high					
24. A positive learning environment is provided in the classrooms					
25. Opportunities for students to work together are provided					
26. The staff have high expectations for all students					
Building community					
27. Teachers and students work together					
28. This is a friendly school					
29. People treat each other with respect at this school					
30. I feel I belong at this school					
31. I trust the staff					
Communication and conflict resolution					
32. I am treated fairly at the school					
33. I am taught to handle conflict respectfully					
34. Staff tell me how I am going with my work					
35. I know what is happening at school					
36. The school rules are consistently applied					
Staff					
37. My teachers are happy					
38. Staff take on various leadership roles					
39. Staff want to help me					
40. Staff at this school are enthusiastic					
41. Staff work well together					
Events/Celebrations/Traditions					
42. The school has traditions and rituals that are celebrated					
43. The school has special events and customs					
44. Achievement is recognised and celebrated					
45. Students are encouraged to contribute					
46. There are opportunities for students to perform and represent the school					

REPRODUCIBLE

Appendix C: School Culture Survey for Students

Instructions – Please answer all questions by ticking the most appropriate number. There are no right or wrong answers.	1	2	3	4	5
Artefacts and physical environment					
47. Cultural and sporting achievements are on display					
48. The school grounds are attractive					
49. There are visible symbols that clearly state what is viewed as important					
50. The facilities are clean and tidy					
Perceptions/Thinking/Feeling					
51. This is a caring school					
52. The teachers provide a positive classroom environment					
53. Staff are always working with me to improve my results					
54. The staff care about me					
55. My teachers encourage me to achieve my personal best					

56. What aspects of your school are great?

57. Can you list three things that you would like to happen that are not currently happening at the school?

Thank you for your time in completing this survey.

REPRODUCIBLE

About the Author

Dr Michael Stewart is a school principal on the Sunshine Coast, Queensland. He recently completed his thesis: *Cultivating a Positive School Culture in a Secondary School Setting: The Principal's Role*. He also has a Master of Educational Administration and Master of Gifted Education. Michael has taught in South Australia, Victoria and Queensland and been a teacher in state, independent and Catholic systems. Michael is a Fellow of the Institute of Managers and Leaders and was awarded the inaugural *Not for Profit* Manager of the Year.

Michael has a record of greatly improving low-performing schools. At the beginning of his first year as a school principal, his school was among the lowest-performing schools in Victoria. After two years the school was awarded consecutive State Literacy Awards. During his second principalship, the school posted above-average improvements in NAPLAN scores three years in a row from the Australian Curriculum, Assessment and Reporting Authority. The school was ranked among the top performing in Australia.

He has presented many workshops at various educational conferences and for large organisations including: Commonwealth Bank; FoodWorks; Mater Misericordiae Hospital; Queensland Police and CQ University. He has a passion for improving teams and leadership performance. Michael brings a great wealth of practical knowledge on how to move organisations forward, especially bringing out the best in individuals.

Michael walks the talk, and has a passion for learning and pursuing challenges. He has studied in Israel and participated in an agricultural exchange program to Sweden for a year. For two years, he worked as a dive instructor on the Great Barrier Reef, winning a tourism award in the process. Michael has also worked in the kitchen at Hungarian and French restaurants. In his younger days, he worked as a gymnastics instructor and swim coach. Michael has a pilot's licence and his leisure pursuits include flying, painting, kite surfing and scuba diving. He has three teenage children and a wonderful, supportive wife.

References

Alberta Education. (2005). *The heart of the matter: Character and citizenship in Alberta schools.* Edmonton: Learning and Teaching Resources Branch.

Alberta Education. (2008). *Supporting positive behaviour in Alberta schools: A school-wide approach.* Edmonton: Learning and Teaching Resources Branch.

Alvy, H. & Robbins, P. (2005). Growing into leadership. *Educational Leadership. 62*(8), 50–54.

Archdiocese of Canberra and Goulburn Catholic Education Office. (2009). *Leadership framework for school leaders.* Archdiocese of Canberra and Goulburn Catholic Education Office.

Australian Institute for Teaching and School Leadership. (2011). *The Australian professional standards for principals.* Carlton South: Education Services Australia.

Australian Institute for Teaching and School Leadership. (2012). *Australian charter for the professional learning of teachers and school leaders.* Carlton South: Education Services Australia.

Barnett, K. & McCormick, J. (2012). *Leadership and team dynamics in senior executive leadership teams.* Educational Management Administration & Leadership. *40*(6), 653–671.

Barth, R. (2002). The culture builder. *Educational Leadership. 59*(8), 6–12.

Bates, R. (2006). Culture and leadership in educational administration: A historical study of what was and what might have been. *Journal of Educational Administration and History. 38*(2), 155–168.

Beaudoin, M. & Taylor, M. (2004). *Creating a positive school culture: How principals and teachers can solve problems together.* Thousand Oaks, CA: Corwin Press.

Brock, K. & Groth, C. (2003). Becoming effective: Lessons from one state's reform initiative in schools serving low-income students. *Journal of Education for Students Placed at Risk. 8*(2), 167–190.

Brown, R. (2004). School culture and organization: Lessons from research and experience. In R. Cleveland, N. Powell, S. Saddler & T. Tyler. (2009). Innovative environments: The equity culture audit: An essential tool for improving schools in Kentucky. *Kentucky Journal of Excellence in College Teaching and Learning. 7*(6), 50–59.

Bush, T. (2009). Leadership development and school improvement: Contemporary issues in leadership development. *Educational Review. 61*(4), 375–389.

Bush, T., Briggs, A. & Middlewood, D. (2006). The impact of school leadership development: Evidence from the new visions programme for early headship. *Journal of In-service Education. 32*(2), 185–200.

Business in the Community. (2009). *Business action for working well.* Retrieved from http://tinyurl.com/77hp5rx

Bustamante, J. (2009). The culture audit: A leadership tool for assessment and strategic planning in diverse schools and college. *International Journal of Educational Leadership Preparation. 1*(3), 1–5.

Caldwell, B. (2015). What is the role of government in education? *Perspectives on Educational Leadership.* (1), 1–2.

Caldwell, B. & Harris, J. (2008). *Why not the best schools?* Camberwell: ACER Press.

Caldwell, B. & Spinks, J. (2008). *Raising the stakes: From improvement to transformation in the reform of schools.* New York: Routledge.

Catholic Education Diocese of Rockhampton. (2014). *Principal role description.* Rockhampton: Catholic Education Diocese of Rockhampton.

Catholic Education Office, Sydney. (2010). *Catholic schools leadership framework: A vision for development and practice of leadership.* Sydney: Author.

Chen, Y. F. & Tjosvold, D. (2005). Cross-cultural leadership: Goal interdependence and leader-member relations in foreign ventures in China. *Journal of International Management. 11*(3), 417–439.

Chiang, L. (2003). *Shaping positive school culture: Judgements of school administrators.* Paper presented at the Annual Conference of the Mid-Western Educational Research Association, Columbus, Ohio, October 15–18.

Cleveland, R., Powell, N., Saddler, S. & Tyler, T. (2009). Innovative environments: The equity culture audit: An essential tool for improving schools in Kentucky. *Kentucky Journal of Excellence in College Teaching and Learning. 7*(6), 50–59.

Cosgrove, P. (2015) *Opening address.* Keynote address at the Australian Council of Educational Leaders, Sydney.

Corsbie, T. (2014). *Making improvements happen.* Keynote address at the Queensland Education Accord Summit, Brisbane.

Coyle, E. (2008). School culture benchmarks: Bridges and barriers to successful bullying prevention program implementation. *Journal of School Violence. 7*(2), 105–122.

Davis, M. (2009). *Distributed leadership and school performance.* (Unpublished dissertation). Washington: The George Washington University.

Deal, T. & Peterson, K. (2002). *The shaping school culture fieldbook.* San Francisco: Jossey-Bass Publishers.

Deal, T. & Peterson, K. (2009). *Shaping school culture: Pitfalls, paradoxes, and promises.* New York: Jossey-Bass Publishers.

Deal, T. & Peterson, K. (1999). *Shaping school culture: The heart of leadership.* San Francisco: Jossey-Bass Publishers.

Department of Education and Training, Queensland. (2010). *A flying start for Queensland children.* Brisbane: Author. Retrieved from http://deta.qld.gov.au

Department of Education and Training, Queensland. (2014). *Queensland Education Accord Summit: Pre-summit preparation.* Brisbane: Author.

Department of Education, Training and Employment. (2013). *Great teachers = Great results: A direct action plan for Queensland schools.* Retrieved from http://deta.qld.gov.au

Devos, G. & Bouckenooghe, D. (2009). An exploratory study on principals' conceptions about their role as school leaders. *Leadership and Policy in Schools. 8*(2), 173–196.

Dimmock, C. & Walker, A. (2005). *Educational leadership: Culture and diversity.* London: Sage Publications.

Dinham, S. (2013). Connecting instructional leadership with clinical teaching practice. *Australian Journal of Education. 57*(3), 220–231.

DuFour, R. & DuFour, B. (2007). What might be: Open the door for a better future. *Journal of Staff Development. 28*(3), 27–28.

Duignan, P. (2013). *Nurturing a collective ethic of responsibility for the leadership of quality learning and teaching in schools.* Sydney: Australian Council for Educational Leaders, Monograph Series, Number 2.

References

Duignan, P. & Cannon, H. (2011). *The power of the many*. Camberwell: Australian Council of Educational Research Press.

Duignan, P. & Gurr, D. (2007). *Leading Australia's schools*. Sydney: Australian Council for Educational Leaders.

Education Review Office. (2008). *Schools' provision for students at risk of not achieving*. Wellington: Author.

Edwards, J. & Martin, B. (2016). *Schools that deliver*. Thousand Oaks: Sage Publications.

Engels, N., Horton, G., Devos, G., Bouckenooghe, D. & Aelterman, A. (2008). Principals in schools with a positive school culture. *Educational Studies. 34*(3), 159–174.

Flaspohler, P. D., Elfstrom, J. L., Vanderzee, K. L., Sink, H. E. & Birchmeier, Z. (2009). Stand by me: The effects of peer and teacher support in mitigating the impact of bullying on quality of life. *Psychology in the Schools. 46*(7), 636–649.

Fredrickson, B. (2009). *Positivity*. Random House, Sydney.

Fullan, M. (2001). *Leading in a culture of change*. San Francisco: Jossey-Bass Publishers.

Fullan, M. (2002). *The change leader*. Educational Leadership, *59*(8), 16–21.

Fullan, M. (2003) *The moral imperative of school leadership*. Thousand Oaks: Corwin Press.

Fullan, M. (2005). *Leadership and sustainability: System thinkers in action*. Thousand Oaks: Corwin Press.

Fullan, M. (2009). *The challenge of change: Start school improvement now! (2nd ed.)*. Thousand Oaks: Corwin Press.

Fullan, M. (2010). *All systems go: The change imperative for whole system reforms*. Thousand Oaks: Corwin Press.

Gaster, R. (2015). *Authenticity and effectiveness: Do as I do, not as I say*. Retrieved from http://www.aim.com.au/blog/authenticity-and-effectiveness-do-i-do-not-i-say

Gillespie, D. (2014). *Free schools*. Melbourne: Pan Macmillan.

Gray, S. & Streshly, W. (2010). *Leading good schools to greatness: Mastering what great principals do well*. Thousand Oaks: Corwin Press.

Guin, K. (2004). Chronic teacher turnover in urban elementary schools. *Education Policy Analysis Archives. 12*(42), 1–30.

Gurr, D. (2014). Finding your leadership. *Perspectives on Educational Leadership*. (3), 1–3.

Gurr, D. (2015). A model of successful school leadership from the international successful school principalship project. *Societies*. (5), 136–150.

Habegger, S. (2008). The principal's role in successful schools: Creating a positive school culture. *Principal. 88(1)*, 42–46.

Hallinger, P. (2003). Leading educational change: Reflections on the practice of instructional and transformational leadership. *Cambridge Journal of Education. 33*(3), 329–351.

Harding, J. (2007). *A study of leadership strategies that promote positive school culture in new high schools*. (Unpublished dissertation). La Verne: University La Verne.

Hargreaves, A. & Fullan, M. (2012). *Professional capital: Transforming teaching in every school*. Cheltenham: Hawker Brownlow Education.

Hargreaves, A. & Shirley, D. (2009). *The fourth way*. Thousand Oaks: Corwin Press.

Harris, A. & Jones, M. (2015). Beyond four walls? Professional learning communities within and between schools. *Australian Educational Leader. 37*(4), 10–12.

Hattie, J. (2009). *Visible learning: A synthesis of over 800 meta analyses relating to achievement.* London: Routledge.

Hattie, J. (2015). Let justice be done, though the heavens fall. *Independent Education. 45*(1), 8–10.

Headsup. (2014). *Creating a mentally healthy workplace: A guide for business leaders and managers.* Retrieved from http://www.headsup.org.au

Helm, C. (2007). Teacher dispositions affecting self-esteem and student performance. *Clearing House. 80*(3), 109–110.

Henderson, M. & Thompson, D. (2003). *Values at work: The invisible threads between people, performance and profit.* Auckland: Harper Collins Publishers.

Hoerr, T. (2006). *The art of school leadership.* Alexandria: Association for Supervision and Curriculum Development.

Holmes, M. (2009). *Creating a positive school culture in newly opened schools.* (Unpublished dissertation). Chapel Hill: North Carolina State University.

James, C. & Connelly, M. (2008). An analysis of the relationship between the organizational culture and the performance of staff work groups in schools and the development of an explanatory model. *International Journal of Leadership in Education. 12*(4), 389–407.

Jensen, B. (2010). *Investing in our teachers, investing in our economy.* Melbourne: Grattan Institute.

Jensen, B. (2014a). *Putting student learning first.* A keynote address at the Queensland Education Accord Summit: Brisbane.

Jensen, B. (2014b). *Turning around schools: it can be done.* Melbourne: Grattan Institute. Retrieved from http://grattan.edu.au/report/turning-around-schools-it-can-be-done/

Jensen, B. & Reichl, J. (2011). *Better teaching appraisal and feedback: improving performance.* Melbourne: Grattan Institute.

Jensen, B., Hunter, A., Lambert, T. & Clark, A. (2015). *Aspiring principal preparation.* Melbourne: Australian Institute for Teaching and School Leadership.

Karakose, T. (2008, May). The perceptions of primary school teachers on principal cultural leadership behaviours. *Educational Sciences: Theory & Practice. 8*(2), 569–579.

Keiser, K. & Schulte, L. (2009). Seeking the sense of community: A comparison of two elementary schools' ethical climates. *The School Community Journal. 19*(2), 45–58.

Kelley, R., Thornton, B. & Daugherty, R. (2005). Relationship between measures of leadership and school climate. *Education. 126*(1), 17–25.

Khalil, U., Kalim, A. & Abiodullah, M. (August 2013). Creating professional school culture through professional development of educational leadership. *Far East Journal of Psychology and Business. 12*(2), 34–54.

King, N. & Horrocks, C. (2010). *Interviews in qualitative research.* Thousand Oaks: Sage Publications.

Kouzes, J. & Posner, B. (2003). *The Leadership Challenge.* San Francisco: John Wiley & Sons.

Lambert, L. (2006). Lasting leadership: A study of high leadership capacity schools. *The Educational Forum. 70*(3), 239–254.

Leithwood, K., Day, C., Sammons, P., Harris, A. & Hopkins, D. (2006). *Seven strong claims about successful school leadership.* London: Department for Education and Skills.

Leithwood, K., Harris, H. & Strauss, T. (2010). *Leading school turnaround: how successful leaders transform low-performing schools.* San Francisco: Jossey-Bass Publishers.

References

Leithwood, K., Seashore Lewis, K., Anderson, S. & Wahlstrom, K. (2004). *How leadership influences student learning*. New York: Wallace Foundation.

Lima, N. (2006). *A case study on principal behaviours cultivating a positive school culture in an elementary school*. (Unpublished dissertation). Rhode Island: Johnson & Wales University Providence.

Marzano, R. J., Waters, T. & McNulty, B. A. (2005). *School leadership that works from research to results*. Alexandria: Association for Supervision and Curriculum Development.

Marzano, R. J. (2015). *High reliability schools: The next step in school reform*. Keynote address at the Australian Council of Educational Leaders, Sydney.

Mascall, B. & Leithwood, K. (2010). Investing in leadership: The district's role in managing principal turnover. *Leadership and Policy in Schools. 9(4)*, 367–383.

Masters, G. (2007). *Restoring our edge in education*. Melbourne: Australian Council for Educational Research.

Masters, G. (2010). *Teaching and learning school framework*. Melbourne: Australian Council for Educational Research.

McGrath, H. & Noble, T. (2010). Supporting positive pupil relationships: Research to practice. *Educational & Child Psychology. 27*(1), 79–90.

McKinsey and Company. 2007. *How the world's best-performing school systems come out on top*. Retrieved from http://www.mckinsey.com/clientservice/social_sector/our_practices/education/knowledge_highlights/best_performing_school.aspx.

Md Nor, S. & Roslan, S. (2009). Turning around at-risk schools: what effective principals do. *The International Journal on School Disaffection. 6*(2), 21–29.

Mercy College. (2013). *Mercy College Mackay: School review and improvement report*. Mackay: Author.

Mercy College. (2014). *An introduction to Mercy College Mackay for new teachers*. Mackay: Author.

Meredith, A. (2009). *Correlational study of union-administrator relationships and principals' opportunities to create positive school culture*. (Unpublished dissertation). Minneapolis: North Central University.

Meredith, A. (2009). *Correlational study of union-administrator relationships opportunities to create positive school culture*. (Unpublished dissertation). Minneapolis: North Central University.

Midlock. S. (2011). *Case studies for educational leadership: Solving administrative dilemmas*. New York: Pearson Education.

Ministerial Council on Education, Employment, Training and Youth Affairs (2008). *Melbourne declaration on educational goals for young Australians*. Retrieved from http://www.mceetya.edu.au/verve/_resources/National_Declaration_on_ the_Educational_Goals_for_Young_Australians.pdf.

Mohe, M. (2008). Bridging the cultural gap in management consulting research. *International Journal of Cross Cultural Management. 8(1)*, 41–57.

Moore, B. (2009). Emotional intelligence for school administrators: A priority for school reform? *American Secondary Education. 37(3)*, 20–28.

Mutch, C. & Collins, S. (2012). Partners in learning: Schools' engagement with parents, families, and communities in New Zealand. *School Community Journal. 22*(1), 167–187.

Nicholas, T. (2015). *Keynote address at the Queensland Education Accord Summit, Brisbane*.

Noonan, J. (2004). School climate and the safe school: Seven contributing factors. *Educational Horizons. 83(1)*, 61–65.

Nuzzi, R., Holter, A. & Frabutt, J. (2012). Mission driven and data-informed leadership. *Catholic Education: A Journal of Inquiry and Practice. 15(2)*, 253–269.

O'Mahony, G., Barnett, B. & Matthews, R. (2006). *Building culture: A framework for school improvement*. Cheltenham: Hawker Brownlow Education.

Ontario Ministry of Education. (2008). *Shaping a culture of respect in our schools: Promoting safe and healthy relationships*. Toronto: Ontario Ministry of Education.

Ontario Ministry of Education. (2010). *Caring and safe schools in Ontario*. Toronto: Ontario Ministry of Education.

Organisation for Economic Co-operation and Development (2005). *Teachers matter: Attracting, developing and retaining effective teachers. (6th ed.)*. Paris: OECD Publishing.

Parsons, J. & Harding, K. (2011). *Making schools work better*. Edmonton: University of Alberta.

Pfeffer, J. & Sutton, R. (2000). *The knowing–doing gap: How smart companies turn knowledge into action*. Boston: Harvard Business School Press.

PricewaterhouseCoopers Australia. (2014). *Creating a mentally healthy workplace: Return on investment analysis*. Retrieved from http://www.headsup.org.au/docs/default-source/resources/beyondblue_workplaceroi_finalreport_may-2014.pdf

Productivity Commission. (2012). *Schools Workforce*. Canberra: Media and Publications.

Raymer, N. (2006). *Principal leadership and school culture in public schools: Case study of two Piedmont North Carolina Elementary schools*. (Unpublished dissertation). Greensboro: University of North Carolina.

Reeves, D. B. (2009). *Assessing educational leaders. Evaluating performance for improved individual and organisational results*. (2nd ed.). Thousand Oaks: Corwin Press.

Rhodes, V., Douglas, S. & Hemings, A. (2011). Creating positive culture in a new urban high school. *The High School Journal. 94(3)*, 82–94.

Robinson, G. (2015). *Will Catholic schools be Catholic in 2030?* In A. Kavanagh & P. Pallisier. (2015). *Will Catholic schools be Catholic in 2013?* Parramatta: Catholic Education Office.

Roffey, S. (2007). Transformation and emotional literacy: The role of school leaders in developing a caring community. *Leading & Managing. 13*(1), 16–30.

Rutledge, S., Cohen-Vogel, L., Osborne-Lampkin, L. & Roberts, R. (2015). Understanding effective high schools: Evidence for personalization for academic and social emotional learning. *American Educational Research Journal. 52*(6), 1060–1092.

Sadlier, H. (2011). Creating and supporting safe and respectful school climates: The principal's role. *The International Journal of Diversity in Organisations, Communities and Nations. 10*(6), 183–197.

Safe Schools Action Team. (2008). *Shaping a culture of respect in our schools: Promoting safe and healthy relationships*. Toronto: Ontario Ministry of Education.

Sahin, S. (2011). The relationship between instructional leadership style and school culture. *Educational Sciences: Theory & Practice. 11(4)*, 1920–1927.

Schein, E. (2004). *Organizational Culture and Leadership*. San Francisco: Jossey-Bass Publishers.

Scott, G. (2003). *Learning principals: Leadership capability and learning research*. Sydney: New South Wales Department of Education and Training, Professional Support and Curriculum Directorate.

Seligman, M. (2011). *Flourish*. North Sydney: Random House Australia.

Senate Standing Committee on Education, Employment and Workplace Relations. (2013). *Teaching and learning – maximising our investment in Australian schools*. Canberra: Senate Printing Unit, Parliament House.

References

Sergiovanni, T. (2006). *The principalship: A reflective practice perspective*. New York: Pearson Education.

Sharp, T. (2014). *Happiness at work with Dr Tim Sharp*. Retrieved from http://blog.aim.com.au/happiness-work-dr-timothy-sharp/

Siccone, F. (2012). *Essential skills for effective school leadership*. New Jersey: Pearson Education.

Sourander, A., Klomek, A. B., Ikonen, M., Lindroos, J., Luntamo, T., Koskelainen, M. & Helenius, H. (2010). Psychosocial risk factors associated with cyberbullying among adolescents. *Archives of General Psychiatry. 67(7)*, 720–728.

Sparks, D. (2009). Reach for the heart as well as the mind: Leaders can take action to close the knowing–doing gap. *Journal of Staff Development. 30(1)*, 48–54.

Stone, K. (2009). *Large North Carolina elementary schools: A qualitative study of school culture and academic achievement.* (Unpublished dissertation). Phoenix: University of Phoenix.

Stronge, J., Richard, H. & Catano, N. (2013). *Qualities of effective principals*. Cheltenham: Hawker Brownlow Education.

Stutz, F. (2015). Tracking rural disadvantage. *Independent Education. 45(1)*, 18–19.

Taylor, C. (2015). *Walking the talk: Building a culture for success*. London: Random House Business Books.

Taylor, J., Jenkins, J. & Barber, L. (2013). *Breaking bad (news): Some constructive criticisms of performance feedback*. Retrieved from: http://www.apaexcellence.org/resources/goodcompany/newsletter/article/481

Tschannen-Moran, M. & Gareis, C. (2004). Principals' sense of efficiency: Assessing a promising construct. *Journal of Educational Administrator. 42(5)*, 573–585.

Turan, S. & Bektas, F. (2013). The relationship between school culture and leadership practices. *Egitim Arastirmalari – Eurasian Journal of Educational Research. 52(1)*, 55–168.

Wagner, C. (2006). School leader's tool. *Principal Leadership. 7(4)*, 41–45.

Waldron, N. & McLeskey, J. (2010). Establishing a collaborative school culture through comprehensive school reform. *Journal of Educational and Psychological Consultation. 20(1)*, 58–74.

Watkins, S. (2005). *An exploration of how some staff members perceive Catholic school renewal in some primary schools in the Catholic Diocese of Rockhampton*. (Unpublished dissertation). Brisbane: Australian Catholic University.

White, D. (2015) *Balancing paradoxes, parables and possibilities*. Keynote address at the ACU: 6th International Conference in Catholic Educational Leadership. Sydney

Zbar, V., Kimber, R. & Marshall, G. (2008). *How our best performing schools come out on top: An examination of eight high-performing schools*. Melbourne: Department of Education and Early Childhood Development.

Zbar, V., Marshall, G. & Power, P. (2007). *Better schools, better teachers, better results*. Camberwell: Australian Council of Educational Research Press.